CHRIST CULTURE:

What the World Needs from the Church
in an Age of Disunity, Disharmony, and Division

Andrew Southwick and Jay Scutt

WESTBOW
PRESS®
A DIVISION OF THOMAS NELSON
& ZONDERVAN

WestBow Press books may be ordered through booksellers or by contacting:

WestBow Press
A Division of Thomas Nelson & Zondervan
1663 Liberty Drive
Bloomington, IN 47403
www.westbowpress.com
1 (866) 928-1240

ISBN: 978-1-9736-4340-1 (sc)
ISBN: 978-1-9736-4342-5 (hc)
ISBN: 978-1-9736-4341-8 (e)

Library of Congress Control Number: 2018912656

Print information available on the last page.

WestBow Press rev. date: 10/25/2018

CONTENTS

A NOTE FROM THE AUTHORS

We (Jay and Andrew) want to thank you for taking the time to read through this book. Our purpose in writing this book is to encourage the church to bring the conversation of cultural reconciliation out of the political and cultural spheres and back onto its proper grounding in scripture. By doing so, we are able to unite people not on the basis of prevailing social thought but on the basis of the gospel.

We readily recognize that there are many churches whose congregations faithfully represent their respective communities, and it would be mistakenly presumptuous to assert that every church everywhere is having trouble ministering across cultural barriers. At the same time, we know that many churches desperately want to bring the gospel to everyone in their communities, but they may not know how to bridge some of the initial chasms they face, and in many cases, one of those chasms is that of heritage and/or culture.

In this book, we examine the good and the bad in terms of the evangelistic efforts of the American church. We also examine the good and the bad in terms of our secular culture, and how we, as a nation, have made strides in the arena of cultural unity. We look at these things not to re-litigate the past, and not find blame, but to help demonstrate our broader argument that the church has not, at least not in its majority, addressed the issue of cultural differences from a gospel-centered perspective. While the church does take seriously the culture gaps in America, and in its own congregations, many of the efforts to inspire unity across such lines are rooted in politics, social efforts, and sometimes guilt.

But what about the gospel?

We believe the reason such cultural gaps exist in the majority of

Christian churches today is because we (Christians) have addressed this issue from the world's perspective, not God's. So it is our goal to present the suggestion to the church that we begin to renew our minds and approach people of all nations and cultures according to the gospel first. The truth is that if we are going to reach people in and through Christ, then we need to reach *people* in and through Christ. When the church addresses cultural divides on any other foundation other than Jesus Christ, the end result is a pandering to some aspect of a person's creation, instead of calling creation *back* to its Creator.

The Bible is clear. Salvation and life are found only in Jesus Christ, and therefore, true unity can only be experienced through Jesus Christ. This, in effect, is Christ Culture, and we are truly grateful to be an encouragement to you, your church, and/or your community.

Sincerely,
Pastor Jay Scutt and Pastor Andrew Southwick

INTRODUCTION

In recent days, the American church has awoken to a serious problem within its current manifestation of ministry: the church is not reaching outside of its own culture groups in America. In other words, the affluent, mostly white church in the suburbs largely keeps its ministry in the suburbs and rarely ventures into the downtown areas. At the same time, black, Hispanic, Asian, and other churches stay largely within their own cultural and ethnic people groups. And while America as a nation has made tremendous strides for equality and civil justice socially, the church, for whatever reason or for a variety of reasons, is slow in making that a reality.

The church has responded to this problem in different ways, all the while trying to right the ship, so to speak. The church has held numerous community outreach services days, which have proved good but not effective in breaching the long-term cultural divide because these efforts usually only last a day or so, and as a result they do not promote long-term relational connection. The church has held rallies and conferences to address the lack of ethnically mixed churches in America, which do a lot to raise awareness, but again, very little in terms of actually breaching the cultural walls in our cities. And of course, the tried and true encouragement to "reach-out-to-someone-who-looks-different-than-you" Christianese forced friendship activity is about as effective at making cross-cultural inroads as trying to buy a cola that doesn't taste like carbonated dirt water from your local health food store.

Socially and politically, the answer to the cultural divides that persist in America is the idea of multi-culturalism. Multi-culturalism is defined as, "the view that cultures, races, and ethnicities, particularly those of minority groups, deserve special acknowledgement of their differences within a dominant political culture."[1] To a growing degree in the church, the idea of multiculturalism is being adopted and tried as yet another solution to the culture chasms between communities and the churches that serve them.

Christ culture proposes a different strategy that finds its basis in contrasting God's intention for humanity with what popular culture has suggested is right. Christ culture encourages Christians to see others as God has created them, regardless of how social culture may present them. This is distinct from merely pursuing multiculturalism because, while Christ culture honors our individual and ethnic cultures, it invites every culture to come under one, larger cultural umbrella—that of Christ Jesus. And that umbrella is shared through the gospel message of Jesus Christ.

We firmly believe that God knew what He was doing when He created humanity and that He knows best how we are to live together in a world that is infected with sin. And the temptation that the church must avoid in America is to place a message of race, color, or culture reconciliation above the message of the gospel of salvation in Christ. Furthermore, we also believe that God knows just how the church is supposed to combat the evils of ethnic preference and racism, and that God demonstrated that strategy in and through the establishing of the church in Acts, and the articulation of the church's distinctives throughout the New Testament. We do not believe that God's design for humanity is to bring us all together only to keep us separated in our cultural corners. Rather, we believe that it is God's intention to bring us all together and adopt us into a brand-new gospel-centered culture— that is, Christ culture.

We invite you to journey with us over these next pages as we endeavor to present a renewing of our minds with respect to how we address and approach racial and cultural relations in America as the church. To be sure, this book is not intended to be a "how to" book, nor do we pretend to have the specific answer that will work in your particular community. But there are some basic principles and truths that God revealed in His word that are applicable throughout the entirety of God's church.

As we endeavor through this book, we will first examine how

---

[1] https://www.britannica.com/topic/multiculturalism. Accessed on 4/25/2018.

the world has attempted to address ethnic and cultural issues. After having surveyed this matter, we will spend the rest of the journey discovering how the early church bridged the culture gaps of their day and draw from those examples the principles that Christians today can apply in their own lives and through their churches in their respective communities.

At its core Christ culture challenges Christians everywhere to see those in their community as God has initially created them. This means that instead of blindly accepting the prevailing social definitions and caricatures that many are quick to identify with, believers must learn to see all people as they are identified by God, going back to His intended purposes for created humanity, and His commands for how we are to treat each other in a sin fallen world.

It is our strong conviction that until the Christian church in America is willing to see people through God's lens, as opposed to the lens of society, the church will continue to falter in its cross-cultural reconciliation efforts. However, by opening our eyes to God's defining of people, and by reaching out to people according to who they are as one of God's creations, the American church can be a glimpse of the glory of heaven as people from every nation stand together worshiping God and loving each other, free from pretense, preconditions, or finite human preferences. This is Christ culture.

CHAPTER I

HONEST CONFESSION: MARTIN LUTHER KING JR. WAS RIGHT

> We must face the fact that in America the church is
> still the most segregated major institution in America.
> At 11:00 a.m. on Sunday morning when we stand and
> sing and Christ has no east or west, we stand at the most
> segregated hour in this nation. This is tragic.
> —Dr. Martin Luther King, Jr.

More than fifty years ago, Dr. Martin Luther King Jr. held a mirror up to the face of the Christian church in American and boldly asserted that the Sunday morning church hour is the most segregated hour in America. While we are not old enough to have lived through the social turbulence of 1960s America, we can certainly see through the lens of history that Dr. King's statement was true of that time. When Dr. King made this claim, America was embroiled in a civil rights battle that was based on the color of people's skin, and the tragic irony was that while secular America was fighting over whether people of different skin color could drink from the same water fountain, the church in America was fighting over whether people of different skin color could worship Jesus from the same pews. And what is perhaps most unsettling about the aforementioned quote is that if one is to properly and thoroughly examine the words of Dr. King, it becomes clear that, at least according to King, the segregation demonstrated in the church was worse than that of secular American culture.

Of course, that was the 1960s, and America has certainly advanced and improved socially from that point in history. Our civil laws have been changed to reflect a growing understanding of the basic humanity of people of all colors and backgrounds, and the lawful segregation that had been a part of America for her first two hundred years has been rightfully overturned. Surely in today's society, without the social and/ or legislative pressure to conform to segregation, the church would be at the forefront of ethnic inclusion and be a beacon to the world when it comes to how all people, regardless of background, can live together and love and support each other. Yet, sadly, that is not the case.

A recent Lifeway survey showed that less than 15 percent of all the churches in America are as ethnically inclusive as other secular institutions (such as: schools, businesses, etc.).[2] In other words, if a given community had and equal percentage representation of ethnic backgrounds, less than 15 percent of the churches in that community would have a congregant population that matches the community integration. The truth is that the large majority of churches in America are made up of one primary ethnic/cultural group, and what's worse is that the majority of people who attend those churches do not sense the need to reach out to anyone beyond their own cultural group.[3] These findings demonstrate that for all the integrated advancement of American society, the church is, for whatever variety of reasons, lagging woefully, neglectfully, and regrettably behind.

Now, if you think even a little bit like we do, you are probably lining up the idea of segregation with race and skin color. And why not? According to popular culture, some of the greatest human divides that exist are between people of different skin colors. And certainly, when we looked around at several church congregations in our local communities

---

[2] Bob Smietana, "Sunday Morning in America Still Segregated – and That's Ok With Worshipers" found on http://lifewayresearch.com/2015/01/15/sunday-morning-in-america-still-segregated-and-that's-ok-with-worshipers/. Accessed on 11/9/17.

[3] Ibid.

and observed a dire lack of multinational representation, our minds went to the ongoing problem of racism at first.

In all candor, this is the second full writing of the introduction for this book. The first introduction that was written focused quite a bit more on the problem of racism in setting up the scene for what will unfold throughout this book. But as we (Jay and Andrew) read back through the middle chapters, we saw that to pigeon-hole the underlying problem on mere skin color would be a shallow and superficial solution to a much deeper problem.

Looking for the Footprints

One of my (Andrew) favorite television shows is *Law & Order*. Every episode is a crime-solving adventure with a closing ethical dilemma that is meant to make the viewer question their presupposed conclusions about whatever case was presented on the show. I took a similar journey while researching for this book. Instead of accepting the easy answer that racism is a problem, and as a result, seek only to achieve reconciliation between skin colors, I wanted to discover where racism came from. How did we as a people end up drawing character conclusions about other people from nothing more than the hues of their skin? And how is it that in a country such as America, with the freedoms and opportunities that we have, something like racism could still plague us to this day, especially since the days of slavery and Jim Crow laws are behind us?

Now, this may sound a bit counterintuitive at first, but stay with me. One of the reasons that social ills such as racism remain an issue in our culture is because we have not effectively followed the footprints of racism to see where it comes from to address its source. In other words, we, as a society, have put so much energy into addressing racism as an isolated symptom that we have failed to accurately address its broader, and more potent, source. Just like the detectives on *Law & Order* when they are assigned a murder case, they do not set out to address murder itself; they look for the murderer. Why? Because if they capture the murderer, it will put an end to that particular strain of evil and allow justice the opportunity to fully prevail. I suggest that taking a likewise approach to something like racism—that is, tracing its footsteps back to its source will go a long way toward helping us as a people overcome such hostile discriminations and learn in ever-increasing measure to live together on this earth. Furthermore, it is the belief of the authors of this book that the Christian church is both uniquely and especially equipped to be able to lead the charge against injustices like these, and in so doing, become a model that the rest of the world can look to and follow.

As will be examined in the forthcoming chapters of this book, the problem of social cancers such as racism can be traced back to three fundamental and underlying causes in contemporary culture.

1)   Racism is not a skin problem; it's a sin problem.

At its absolute core, racism is a product of sin. In the next chapter, we will look at sin's entrance into the world and its resulting effects on how human beings both view and treat each other. The underlying sin that gives force to racism is pride—the sinful idea that one person's world, views, and existence is inherently better and greater than that of another. This tension creates a war of personal sovereignties, and nowhere in created history can two ultimate sovereignties coexist. Instead, one sovereignty must be, and is inevitably, defeated by the other. In human examples, this has resulted in the senseless bloodshed of millions upon millions of people around the world who died for no other reason than they were considered to be less human than someone else, for whatever reason, be it skin color, religion, etc.

It is precisely because of the above that the Christian church has such a unique place in the area of justice throughout the world. Christians believe that Jesus Christ conquered sin and death through His own sacrificial death on the cross, and resurrection three days later, and that Jesus has given to the church the ministry of reconciliation (2 Corinthians 5:11–21). Said reconciliation is first and foremost a work of evangelism—that is, pointing people to life in Christ—and second, as a result of a person's life in Christ and adoption into the family of Christ, the reconciliation happens between people as well. It is only the Holy Bible, and only Jesus Christ, who taught and demonstrated that victory over sin does not happen by human effort, but by the work of God in

Christ and through the Holy Spirit. Therefore, theologically speaking, if racism is at its root a sin problem, then it must be addressed as such, and fought with the appropriate weapons, which the Bible tells us is God's word and the person and work of Jesus Christ.

2) Skin color has been confused to indicate character and human worth.

When I (Andrew) was growing up, I collected baseball cards. I had quite an extensive collection, yet the vast majority of my cards were not worth the paper on which they were printed. Baseball cards derive their value from a variety of ever-shifting and subjective factors. While a card that features one of the all-time greats will be worth something, it is only worth that something if there is another buyer willing to pay that price. The rest of a card's value is all about its looks, conditions, and printing, essentially, and all those factors are determined by certain baseball card experts, called graders, who bestow various values on all kinds of baseball cards. There is no way to pinpoint exactly what a card is worth in the same way that one might be able to closely estimate the cost of a gallon of milk because of the sliding grading scale used to grade and evaluate baseball cards. The exact same card held by two or more people could all fetch different amounts at auctions or from other collectors, again, depending on a host of factors.

Over time, skin color has been confused to be an indicator of a person's character and worth, much like how a baseball card's condition is judged to determine its value. And just like a baseball card, there are a variety of ever-changing criteria that people have used to assign certain values to those who look different and/or live differently than they do. Quickly, what gives a person their value? Think of some things that you believe give a person their value. I (Andrew) have asked many Christians this very question and the main answer they give is that a person gets their value from God. Of course, I agree wholeheartedly with this answer, especially since the secular world's evaluation of intrinsic human value is tied to the person's perceived quality of life (i.e., one justification used to support the practice of abortion is the idea that the unborn child will not have a good quality of life), and/or what said person will be able to contribute to society. In fact, there are entire economic philosophies based upon a person's value *to society*, which is distinct and altogether different from a person having value and worth simply because he or she is a person. From a generally accepted secular humanistic worldview, a person's value is based on their worth to the society as a whole, and from a generally accepted biblical perspective, a person gets their value from God; in other words, God gives the person value.

Again, we agree that God does give a person value, but we also think it is important to take that statement a step further. Speaking biblically, a person has value because *people are valuable to God*. You see, to say that a person has value because God gives them value, while true in one sense, still leaves open the idea that a person in their basic state has no value unless value is imputed to them. On the other hand, the Bible teaches us that people have value because people are valuable to God. People are so valuable to God that, instead of God making us pay for our sin (which we could not do in the first place), God stepped in and paid the price Himself through the person of Jesus Christ. Furthermore, with respect to the value that God gives us, that can be seen in the very foundation of the creation of humankind wherein God created people in His image (Genesis 1:27). God did not sacrifice Himself for *any other aspect of creation* except for people. Such a revelation illustrates that every person has value because every person is pricelessly and eternally valuable to God.

Sadly, for most of the world, and most of America, whether or not people are indeed valuable to God is of no consequence. Perhaps that is because so many people reject God and therefore would not want to have any value that is related to Him. Or maybe it is prejudice that has been passed down through generations, or maybe it is one's own selfishness that causes one to grade a person's value like a baseball card. Regardless of the reason, humanity has done a spectacular job at separating people into competing demographics and then nicknaming them according to the color of their skin. Without question, such compartmentalization of people has only served to damage human interaction and severely fracture the welfare of families, neighborhoods, and communities worldwide.

3) A person's skin color has been conflated with his or her culture

This is point that establishes the context for this entire book, and this is also the point upon which we (Jay and Andrew) will spend the most time in examination. Throughout world history, people have unjustly discriminated against one another. For most of history, such discrimination was not based on skin color, but upon one's nationality or direct genetic-ethnic heritage. It is only within the last thousand years that skin color has become so inextricably linked to how people view and value each other. Nonetheless, we, as a people, have errantly confused a person's skin color with a person's culture, and it is this confusion, I submit, that has led to the racism that has existed in the past and that we understand exists today.

While sin is the ultimate foundational layer of discriminatory injustice, the confusing of skin color and culture provides the next layer. When examining the history of racism in America, one will soon see a pattern of cultural fear emerge. Such cultural fear is what drives racism. Cultural fear is the idea that another person's culture is a threat to my own culture, and since I do not want my own culture to be overtaken, I will resist and fight the new and threatening culture at all costs. In the confusion of skin color and culture, people have time and again tried to socially engineer the "perfect society" by eliminating the elements of human culture that they thought to be of lesser value. The late Margaret Sanger, the founder of Planned Parenthood, is a famous example of this idea. She was fearful of what she deemed to be the "lesser" people of society eventually overtaking the "better" people of society, and so she sought to achieve her goal of protecting and fostering a perfect society by biologically and genetically eliminating the "lesser beings" of the world.[4] As the rise of ideas such as those of Margaret Sanger became more and more commonplace in Western society, color became synonymous with culture.

When color is seen, taught, and understood as a predictor of culture, a whole host of new problems emerge. First, and most obviously,

---

[4] Jerry Bergman, *Birth Control Leader Margaret Sanger: Darwinist, Racist, Eugenist* found on https://creation.com/margaret-sanger-darwinian-eugenicist. Accessed on January 22, 2018.

judgments about people become sweeping and general in nature. For instance, what aspects of culture do you most closely associate with Caucasian people? What kinds of culture do you most closely associate with black people? What about Hispanics, or Asians? Objectively speaking, I (Andrew) am confident that many Christians today would agree that a person's skin color does not dictate or predetermine the kind of culture that they would live in and/or practice. Nonetheless, the mental image is still there. I submit that this is societal conditioning, accomplished largely through commercial mass marketing, that has been accepted by the public. In reality, there are multiple expressions of varying cultures within a given society, and skin color does not determine which culture, or expression of culture, a person will experience/exhibit. Granted, a person's skin color can provide small clues as to a person's genetics, and with lesser accuracy, a general idea of where said person may come from (i.e., darker people tend to live in, or be from sunnier climates, while lighter people tend be from geographic locations with less direct sunlight), but even this tells us that the color of someone's skin is influenced by *other factors*, as opposed to the color of a person's skin *influencing* the surrounding factors of their life.

Another problem that comes with using skin color as a culture predictor is the friction that is created when a particular culture is seen as a threat to another culture. It is when skin color is confused with culture at this stage, that we can readily see how laws mandating segregation became the norm in America for centuries. As Americans, we naturally want American culture to thrive, but instead of welcoming and assimilating other cultures into our own, we segregated those cultures that we saw as dangerous to the American way of life. And since we wrongly connected skin color with culture, the laws of segregation were based on the skin color(s) that were thought to be the biggest cultural threats.

To be sure, when it comes to culture wars, the church has succumbed to errant understandings as well. Just because we might be a Christian does not mean that we are also not human, and certainly, Christians have waged culture wars among themselves, and among, and even against, their own communities. The problem facing the church concerning cultural reconciliation and assimilation is that the church has gotten too used to self-segregating the kinds of cultures within itself. Such dividing represents a kind of abdication of the church's biblical mandate to make disciples of all nations (Matthew 28:19). Simply put, cultural reconciliation and assimilation is incredibly difficult, and rife with discomfort, uneasiness, and tension. The early church experienced this in their everyday lives (as well as during their worship gatherings), yet the Jews and Gentiles in the early church were faithful in learning how to fully worship together, not just at separate times under the same roof, or in separate parts of their communities.

In recent years, there have been cries from Christians and church leaders for the American church to see the error of these ways and to return to ministry of reconciliation that the apostle Paul wrote about in 2 Corinthians. Up to the present day, the way that the church has dealt with assimilating different cultures is by giving said culture its own space at church that does not upset the preexisting culture that is already there. This approach is seen in things as trivial as music style all the way to literal culture-specific church services. Here again, on one hand, this is a good thing. After all, churches need to welcome those who live in their communities regardless of culture. However, this approach is also a kind of self-segregation that prevents the church from learning how to share their culture with people of a different culture. It is easy for a long-established American church to welcome a new Spanish church by having them meet during off hours in a spare classroom or a multipurpose room. It is quite another thing for that same established American church to expand their culture bandwidth to include that of the new Spanish church at the same time, at the same place, and in the same worship service. But it is just this kind of culture-expanding adoption that we (Jay and Andrew) believe that the church needs to return to.

As pastors, Jay and I see many Christian ministry trends pop up as time moves forward. Christianese church buzz-words like *missional*, *authentic*, and *relational* become hallmarks of ministry movements in the Christian church. Currently, the church's big buzzword mission focus is *multicultural*, meaning that the Christian church sees that it is embarrassingly segregated, and there is a renewed and intentional desire to change that. Now I understand the goal of the church's current focus on being multi-cultural, but the question must be raised: Is it enough for the Christian church to simply have people of different cultures and skin colors in mere attendance, or is there another layer of integration that should occur?

We suggest that there is another layer of integration that is needed if the church is to effectively desegregate and become effective at reaching across cultural lines within local communities in America. It is true that the church needs to shift from a mono-cultural approach to a multicultural approach when it comes to ministry, but once at the multicultural stage, the church must continue into Christ culture, because it is in Christ culture that we are intended to live. From the beginning of the creation of humankind, God has been in the business of bringing different and distinct cultures together and transforming them into one new culture that is comprised of the best of each culture that is in the mix, so to speak.

God first turned the multicultural into Christ culture when Adam and Eve were brought together and became one (Genesis 2:23–25). In creating people, God created men and women. Both are inherently valuable, both are of the highest eternal worth, both are positionally equal with each other, and yet men and women are distinct in personality, in how they relate to each other, in how they problem solve, and in how they view the world. It is certain that anyone who has been, or is, married, has experienced the world-changing mind-set shift of learning to live and love one's spouse. Marriage was the first example of two cultures coming together and learning a new culture—Christ culture. Fast forward to the early church and the letters of the apostle Paul in the New Testament. Virtually all of Paul's letters deal with the new Christian church learning to worship Jesus and live life with people who were of a different culture (i.e. Jews and Gentiles learning to worship God and live life together, not at separate times and in separate rooms, etc.). Was this difficult for church to do? Absolutely. But was this a part of the original mission of the church? Again, absolutely. And it is precisely this part of the original mission of the church that has been missing among us for far too long.

You see, culture transcends color, and it is the relational culture wars that divide people to this day. Those culture wars may be blamed on various physical characteristics, but underneath all the sensational headline-making reasons, it is about the clash of different cultures. Throughout world history, different cultures have been perceived to be threatening toward each other, and in our human pride, we elevate our own national and personal cultures as the high-water mark of humanity. In other words, when another culture presents itself to us, we first evaluate whether their culture is a threat to our own, and if we believe it is (a threat), historically, we have responded with more and more isolation, and, at times, genocidal extermination.

As we continue through this book, we will examine briefly the problem of racism, but the majority of our focus will be on the idea of Christ culture—what Christ culture is, and how the church can bring Christ culture to their own communities. As we will see in the forthcoming chapters, it is the intention of Jesus Christ to bring all those who will believe in Him from all nations and cultures, and through Him and in Him, make them one culture and one nation. As we move forward in this book, we (the authors) will pull no punches when it comes to the responsibility of the church in bringing to the world, Christ culture. Of course, it is not our intention for this to become an excuse to de-constructively criticize the church, or the church's efforts thus far concerning the culture wars in America. Nor is it our intention to re-litigate the painful effects of racial division and/or impugn society's efforts to address prejudice. Rather, our intention is to provide a suggested solution that will enable those *temporary* efforts of racial and cultural reconciliation to become *permanent* parts of the DNA of the church. We will take a look at what a "race" really is, and ask the question, "Is there really more than one race of people?" Furthermore, we will richly and thoroughly examine Christ culture as it is taught and demonstrated in the Bible and connect Christ culture to the church and its God-given mission to disciple all nations, so the American church might be reignited and inspired to invite all people not just to church on Sunday but into Christ culture every day.

CHAPTER 2

WHAT IS CHRIST CULTURE? GETTING BACK TO THE FUTURE

C hrist culture is God's intended design for human relations. Christ culture is not just an ideal that was meant for heaven, but it was what God created in the garden of Eden in the first place. In fact, the story of the Bible, the beautiful story of Christ's redeeming and saving work that accomplished the reconciliation of people to Himself through faith in Him alone is the middle section of a journey of history, time, and eternity that ends with a new version of the original beginning. In other words, what God intended for creation and humankind in the beginning, He will once again restore, and all those who put their faith on Jesus will inherit the right to partake in that restored perfection with Jesus forever. So in the beginning, before sin came into the world, Christ culture was the way of living for all people, but sadly, only two people (hint: Adam and Eve) would ever know what that would be like, since it was those two people who would fall to temptation and allow sin to woefully infect the whole world and every person who would ever live in the world from that day forward. Nonetheless, what God intended in the beginning, He intends to restore and sustain for eternity.

With the aforementioned as a starting point, how then can Christ culture be experienced in the here and now? After all, if Christ is restoring it for eternity, would it not be impossible to achieve before that time? Well, yes and no.

The impossibility of achieving what Christ accomplished stems from two primary truths:

1. Since the payment for sin (sinless life, death, and resurrection) was something only Christ could do, then people are necessarily incapable of doing it themselves. In other words, only God can do what only God can do.

2. A primary distinctive of the ultimate fulfillment of Christ's redeeming and reconciling work is that people would live in new created earth wherein sin would no longer be present, and since sin is present in this world, that also prevents humankind from realizing the fullest effects of Christ culture.

With that said, there are parts of Christ culture that can be accomplished here on earth, and that were and are mandated by the church to carry out (see introduction for scripture references). Christ culture, in its basic idea, is that all people, regardless of national heritage or particular ethnicity would populate and share a common world, all sustained by God Himself. In this common world, there is no so such thing as currency. There is a common language, and life is a shared experience both with God and with other people. But let's not take our word for it. Let's look at the evidence that the Bible provides for us.

God Meant to Do What He Meant to Do

To better understand Christ culture, we need to first understand God's intention for human relations, and to understand God's intention for human relations, it is helpful to gain a broader perspective into God's process of creation.

The first and most important context of creation to grasp is that God created the garden of Eden to be a type (or perhaps a foreshadowing) of tabernacle wherein His creation, humanity, would delight (the name, Eden, means *delight*) in not only the land in which they lived, but also in the unfettered relationship between humanity and God, and between each other.[5] The aforementioned truth tells us that God intended for humanity to live in harmony with Him and with each other, and on top of all of that, God wanted humanity to delight together in the whole of creation as well. The whole earth that God created was created with humanity in mind. God was careful, intentional, and thorough in creating a world that would supply people's physical needs, while being a true place of joy for His upcoming creation.

Of particular note is the fact that nowhere in the description of creation does God create "nations," "races," or other such ethnic divisions. The Bible simply tells us that God created the earth and then created humans. Then God placed the humans in the garden of Eden and gave them every good blessing imaginable (and some that we cannot imagine because our minds are infected and veiled by sin, and prior to sin's introduction into the world, Adam and Eve's minds were perfect). Additionally, and in stark contrast to the evolutionary theory that humankind developed its various languages over millions of years, it is clear from the account of creation that humanity could communicate linguistically with each other and with God from the very beginning, thus supplying evidence to the fact that God initially only gave humanity one language. The commonalities seen in the creation account indicate that God's intention was not for humankind to be organized into separate people groups based on skin color and/or nation of origin, those kinds of divisions came later and were consequences of sin's presence and influence in the world.

The importance of God's intention for humanity cannot be understated. The objection is sometimes offered, "How can anyone attempt to understand God's intentions for creation if they weren't there in the first place?" While it is true that no mortal, finite-minded person can presume to know how God's mind works, we can glean some conclusions based on the fact that humankind was created in God's image (Genesis 1:27). Since God is a spirit, and therefore does not have a physical body, we must conclude that to be created in God's

---

[5] Gaebelein, F. E., Sailhamer, J. H., Kaiser, W. C., Jr., Harris, R. L., & Allen, R. B., Zondervan Pub. House. (1990). *The Expositor's Bible Commentary: Genesis, Exodus, Leviticus, Numbers* (Vol. 2). Grand Rapids, MI: Zondervan Publishing House.

image does not refer to our physical image, but our spiritual, mental, and emotional image. For example, our need for relationship is born out of God's relational nature (again, Genesis 1:27). Our abilities to reason and speak articulately are also aspects of God's nature. Our ability to love, weigh options, care, and feel joys and sorrows are all parts of God's "image" that He imparted to humanity.

So it is reasonable to draw a connection between humankind's ability to be intentional, and God's intentional nature. Humans' ability to be intentional is a part of God's nature that He shared with humanity at creation. And when we examine our reasons for being intentional, it is not outside the bounds of theological fidelity to assert that God has reasons for being intentional as well, and that some of those reason can be gleaned from His revealed truth, which is the Holy Bible.

I (Andrew) remember when my wife and I were about to celebrate our second Christmas as a married couple together, I wanted to really make it a memorable holiday. I hatched a plan about six weeks before Christmas to get my wife's engagement ring and take it to the jeweler to confirm its size so that I could buy her a companion ring. I had a whole grandiose scheme with which to give my wife her Christmas gift as well. I would first establish a ruse in order to get my wife to give me her ring to take to the jeweler without arousing suspicion (I told her I was going to get it cleaned, which was true also). Then, while the ring was with the jeweler, I would choose a companion ring and give both to her for Christmas.

At this time in our marriage, we were living in a small, second-floor, two-bedroom apartment about an hour north of Seattle, Washington. As most apartments do, our apartment had a set of concrete stairs that went up to our front door. When Christmas week finally came, I waited until she went to work to put my plan into its final stages. First, I placed a series of Hershey's Kisses chocolates on each one of the stairs that led to our front door, and going into our apartment. Then I took rose petals and made a floral bedding for the two small boxes that contained her rings. At the front of the rose petal bedding, I placed a card that read, "Now that I've kissed"—Get it? The Hershey's Kisses?—"the ground you walk on, will you marry me again?" After this, I went to the jeweler to pick up the rings, and finally I arranged to meet Rebecca in the parking lot of our apartment complex, so that I could then take her out to dinner, thus saving the reveal of the whole plan for the night's grand finale.

Everything was perfect. My plan was going off without a hitch. Our neighbors, who would come and go throughout the evening, left the chocolates on the stairs, and dinner was great. It was time for the piece de resistance. As we drove home from dinner, my pulse rose, and I could feel my nerves start to run laps in world record time around my body. I was so hoping that this gift would be memorable, exciting, and an incredible picture of how much I loved my wife. It wasn't until we pulled into our parking space that I realized that I had forgotten to take the rings out of the car and put them on the rose petal bedding, which meant the rings were in the car with us, and not in the apartment like they were supposed to be!

I could not believe it. Now, instead of getting a beautiful companion ring and testimony of my undying and ever-growing love, bathed in an over-the-top romantic public display of romanticism, my wife was about to walk up the stairs over chocolates that were littered on every step, and into an apartment with a three-by-five notecard laying in a pile of dead flower parts. Oh yes, merry Christmas, my darling. I had to think fast. I needed to get my wife out of the car so I could get rings out of the glove box and put them in my pocket, and then I needed to make it up the stairs and into the apartment before her so I could put the rings on the aforementioned dead flower parts so that they would look like they were there the whole time.

But how could I explain that I needed my wife to get out of the car, and *then* how could I explain why I was about to run away, up the stairs, and into the apartment, while she walked in from the parking lot? I panicked. And in my panic, I said to my wife, "Do you think you could get out of the car and wait by the trunk while I get your rings out of the glove box?"

Yeah. I said that.

I suppose if I had just said "ring," in its singular form, that the whole thing could have been salvaged. But I did not use the singular word form. I said, "rings," in the plural form. It was a word choice my wife picked up on rather quickly. My wife's next three sentences were as follows: "Why are you acting so weird? What do you mean, 'rings'? But seriously, why are you acting so weird?"

"I was trying to surprise you with a companion ring for Christmas," I replied.

"I knew you didn't take my ring just to get it cleaned. Can we go inside now? Its cold outside," my wife answered.

As we walked up the stairs, my wife noticed how someone threw a pack of Hershey's Kisses onto the stairs and wondered who had done that. I told her that I had no idea, and we went inside.

You have probably heard the phrase, "It's the thought that counts." Well, that phrase is talking about a person's intentions. Our intentions matter, and God's intentions matter. I shared the previous story with you to illustrate the importance and clarifying meaning of intention. I was very intentional in what I wanted to accomplish and what I wanted my wife to experience as a result of my efforts. It was not until a horrific lapse in judgment, followed by a series of mistakes, that the *actual* results and my *intended* results differed. The same is true when discerning God's intent for humankind. God had very specific intentions for humankind. He thought the whole thing through. But when a tragic lapse in judgment by Adam and Eve messed everything up, the results differed from God's intentions.

This is why it is critical that we understand what God intended for us as human beings concerning how we relate to one another if we are going to repair the lines of racial division that have plagued us as a people for most of the history of the world. And the first piece of God's intention that we need to grasp is that God created the world with the intention that all people would share it as one race and one nation—His holy nation.[6] But sin messed this all up. Yet God, in His mercy, made a way for His original intentions to be restored and for humankind to be reconciled back to Him to be able to delight once again in a new

---

[6] This does not mean that God was, or is, a Communist or a Socialist or otherwise political (as we understand government through a largely political lens). Communism and Socialism are governmental constructs invented by man. And since God did not institute human government until *after* sin entered the world, we can infer that the government God intended for humankind was His own; a benevolent theocracy of sorts.

and perfect creation that will last forever. It is at this point that we turn to what God is restoring us to in order to shine a brighter light on the definition of Christ culture.

God Brings Humanity Back to the Future

In Revelation 21:1–6, the apostle John describes his vision of the new heavens and new earth that Christ is now preparing for those believe in Him. In his description, John includes three phrases that define God's intention for humankind, and how we are to relate to Him and to one another.

> And I heard a loud voice from the throne saying, "Look! God's dwelling place is now among the people, and he will dwell with them. They will be his people, and God himself will be with them and be their God" (Revelation 21:3 NIV 2011)

To Live in Christ Culture, God Must Live in You

Just like when God prepared this earth, He is preparing a new one, and this time, God's literal dwelling place will be among His people—that is, all those who have placed their faith in the Messiah Jesus Christ. This is a primary attribute of Christ culture because it acknowledges that God dwells among His people. To be sure, while this sin-soaked earth is not the new sin-free earth that God is preparing, there is a picture of this new earth that can be partially demonstrated today.

The apostle Paul teaches us that God, in the person of the Holy Spirit, dwells in every believer (1 Corinthians 3:16). Furthermore, Paul also teaches us that each person is a temple in which God dwells (2 Corinthians 6:16). This means that God has already taken up residence in and among the local church today. The question is, when the people of our respective communities visit our church gatherings, is it obvious that God dwells among us? In answering this question, we need to think beyond they lyrics of our worship songs and the morning message because the evidence of God among us as a church is not simply what we do in our worship centers and auditoriums, but also in what we, as individuals, say in the lobby, how we welcome those who are new to our church family, and the looks that we briefly flash to those who do not look like us. It's how we choose to our seats when someone we do not know has taken their place in our usual spot.

For instance, think of the place where you live. Is it obvious that you live there? What kinds of things around you home point to the fact that you live there? When we talk about living somewhere, we are not talking about evidence that you have been there once or twice, or about the memories of when you used to live there, but what evidence points to you living there right now? Would you like to know the answer? Here it is. The evidence that proves that you live there is the testimony of those who live with you. It would be tempting to say that the evidence of your dwelling is proved by the fact that all your current stuff is there, but that does not necessarily mean that you live there at all. For all anyone knows, you could have left some time ago and no one bothered to move your stuff. Or perhaps you are merely storing your things there and you actually live somewhere else. Certainly, the irrefutable proof that you live there is the fact that the influence of your presence overflows from the lives of those who live with you.

Now think about your church, and be honest. If you were to bring a scale into your church to weigh the amount of God-*stuff that people like* on one side, and the amount of genuine God-overflow *that comes out of His people* on the other, which would be heavier? If we want to be a reflection of Christ culture here on earth, we must overflow His very presence, not just hang His holy knickknacks on our walls. In the new heavens and earth that the apostle John writes about, this will be an automatic thing, especially since sin's presence will be removed (when John writes about there being "no more sea," he is speaking metaphorically about sin's presence being eliminated. The connotations of the "sea" are overwhelmingly evil, as the "sea" is the source of the

Satanic beast and the destination of the dead),[7] but here on earth, the overflowing of God's presence is a result of our humble obedience and submission to Jesus.

> He will wipe every tear from their eyes. There will be no more death or mourning or crying or pain, for the old order of things has passed away. He who was seated on the throne said, "I am making everything new!" (Revelation 21:4–5 NIV 2011)

To Live in Christ Culture, We Must Live in a New Culture

In an upcoming chapter, we will examine the definition of a culture specifically, but for now, we need to emphasize and clarify the idea that Christ culture is a new culture. In other words, a true Christ culture is not a finite human culture. While there certainly are elements of finite human tradition that are a part of Christ culture, Christ culture is those finite elements under the absolute lordship of Christ. The challenge that the church has with this is the fact that we constantly try to establish our own earthly cultures and then try to get God's endorsement for it, instead of discovering His new Christ culture as a people in submission to Him. Of course, it is not that the church necessarily means to do this, but it is a byproduct of our tendency to cling to controllable comforts while at the same time slowly drifting from our mandated mission to make disciples of nations. When these symptoms become a habitual culture, we use the church for our own needs, instead of the church being a body of believers united in Christ and meeting the needs of their community.

What the apostle John wrote in these verses was not the first time that Jesus had said something similar concerning His ushering in a new

---

[7] Johnson, A. F. (1981). Revelation. In F. E. Gaebelein (Ed.), *The Expositor's Bible Commentary: Hebrews through Revelation* (Vol. 12). Grand Rapids, MI: Zondervan Publishing House.

order. The gospels of Matthew, Mark, and Luke all include the parable of the wineskins (Matthew 9:14–17; Mark 2:21–22; Luke 5:33–39).

In short, Jesus was illustrating that He is bringing in an era of "new wine," and that the old wineskin of Judaic tradition would not be able to hold it. The *Expositor's Bible Commentary* explains:

> These illustrations show that the new situation introduced by Jesus could not simply be patched onto old Judaism or poured into the old wineskins of Judaism. New forms would have to accompany the kingdom Jesus was now inaugurating; to try to domesticate him and incorporate him into the matrix of established Jewish religion would only succeed in ruining both Judaism and Jesus' teaching.[8]

My wife and I (Andrew) enjoy quiet evenings at home with a dish of ice cream and a television show. One of our favorite television shows is called *Chopped*. The show features four professional chefs who compete through three rounds of cooking, with their dishes being judged by celebrity chefs who eliminate one chef per round until a winner is selected. Each round features a basket of mystery ingredients that the chefs must use and turn into an outstanding course of food. It never fails to fascinate me how the chefs are able to take those random ingredients and make anything, never mind if it actually tastes good. It seems to me that the average mystery basket usually includes things like Pink Lady apples, chocolate wine, beef tongue, and shredded pieces of tractor tire.

Now, I am not 100 percent sure that those are even real foods, but I do know that if I were presented with that basket of ingredients, all the celebrity chef judges would get to eat from me would be sliced apples seasoned with cinnamon and sugar. As for the other ingredients, I would place them in the trash where they belong. But the chefs who compete on the show take every ingredient and transform it into something new,

---

[8] Carson, D. A. (1984). <u>Matthew</u>. In F. E. Gaebelein (Ed.), *The Expositor's Bible Commentary: Matthew, Mark, Luke* (Vol. 8, p. 227). Grand Rapids, MI: Zondervan Publishing House.

something that was not there before, and that something is far more innovative than sliced apples.

When it comes to the church, Jesus wants to do the same thing with us. And what's more, Jesus has a brand-new life in mind for those who trust in Him, both here on earth and fulfilled in full in eternity. Jesus wants to take ingredients of all kinds, from all nations, and make a beautiful meal (so to speak), something entirely new. However, in our sin brokenness, we do not always offer our ingredients to Jesus to do what He wants to with them. Instead, we offer our ingredients to Jesus on the condition that He makes the meal that we want Him to, the way we want Him to do it, as long as He keeps it pretty much the same. When we do this, we fail to recognize that Jesus does not work like that. Jesus does not respond to our ultimatums and/or demands, even (and perhaps especially) when we try to direct Him in His own name, and He does not leave anything or anyone the same. Jesus is a life changer, and He wants all of us offered back to Him. He wants us to trust Him to do what is best with our ingredients of humanity, mixing them, marinating them, cutting them, peeling them, etc.

One of the reservations that many Christians have about sharing the gospel across racial lines is the fact that they are uncomfortable outside of their own, familiar human finite cultures. When faced with a different culture, it is like trying to mix shredded tractor tires into a meal. For us, it is impossible, but Jesus is the chef that knows how to use all of our "national ingredients" in a beautiful way. Only Jesus can mix the ingredients of all nations together and have them produce a beautiful medley of flavor that benefits the world and brings glory to Him. And we need to understand that when we do not allow Jesus to do this in our churches, we are effectively settling for apple slices with cinnamon and sugar, when we could enjoy so much more in Christ's name.

Christ culture demands that we cease trying to add Jesus to our existing cultures. Instead, we must submit our personal and corporate finite human cultures to Him, and He will lead us into a new culture—a Christ culture.

He said to me: "It is done. I am the Alpha and the Omega, the Beginning and the End. To the thirsty I will give water without cost from the spring of the water of life." (Revelation 21:6 NIV 2011)

To Live in Christ Culture, We Must Not Add Cost to His Culture

Just as is written in John 7 and Romans 3, Jesus again says (through the apostle John) that His salvation is free, and all that one needs to do is to come and drink, and they will inherit eternal life. To be sure, Jesus demands that we sacrifice all that we are in surrender to Him, and such sacrifice is a great cost to us because dying unto self means that we give up what we perceive to be our rights to obey the one who is righteous. The distinction here is that sometimes, we can present an unintentional Pharisee-ism that demands that, for anyone to join our particular fellowship, they must submit to *our* culture by first demonstrating that they are worthy of adoption.

Humankind has a peculiar habit of demanding submission from each other for one person or another (or one group of people or another) to be accepted or otherwise included. It is peculiar because people, at their default mode, despise having to submit to anyone or anything, yet the same people who despise it for themselves demand that other people submit to their preferences, rules, regulations, and personal cultures. Take the action of driving, for example. I would stake a small fortune on the fact that many people in America can, will, and likely have complained about that "idiot driver" that almost cut them off on the freeway, or who was driving too slow, or who was on their phone while driving, etc. Along with that, if those people are like me, they probably think that if people would just drive more like them, that there would never be any accidents, or traffic jams, or anything else of the kind. Yes, driving everywhere would be a breeze if people would only drive the way I do. This is a simple, yet (I believe) identifiable example of how many people want every other person to submit to their own standards and practices. And of course, when people do not submit to our standards, or in other words, when they fail to drive the way we do (and/or stay out of our way on the road), we condemn them with vehement hostility. Perhaps not all of us go into a full-on road rage mode, but we do mutter to ourselves a series of curses on the "idiot driver" that even our own mothers would disapprove of if they were to hear such words. Maybe it's only me, but I doubt it.

Here again, the church is not excluded from these tendencies, except in church, it is not to a matter of driving style that Christians demand submission, but to a worship style. In the interest of clarity, when we mention worship style, it is not just music to which we refer, but the entire presentation and practice of "church." A great many churches across America have inadvertently (giving them some benefit of the doubt) crippled their community outreaches because they are unwilling to allow new traditions into their existing church cultures, thereby alienating those in their communities who might bring a different approach to ministry expressions. There is simply no room in most churches in America for change once the church has become "too" established (i.e., used to itself, its habits, and so on), and no willingness to embrace any culture that is not the current, familiar one. If a visitor to a given church desires to be a part of said church, they will be assimilated not just into a certain kind of order in the church, but into that church's own culture. The problem is, that assimilation comes at the expense of the visitor's own culture, and now said visitor feels like they must become a whole new person to fit into this new church.

And by "new person," we are not talking about a new life in Christ that reflects a life more like Christ, but rather a new membership application that requires that said person's life reflect that of the *people in the church* instead of the one upon whom the church is built. Sadly, the oft-repeated mantra of "come as you are" in church only applies to those who "are" already in the club. Otherwise, a visitor needs to "be like them" before they can worship with them.

Having served as music pastors ourselves, we know firsthand how difficult it is for Christians to embrace a new culture of any kind, in any aspect of their church. Rarely a week went by that people in the congregation would tell us how, if we would just lead the good old songs in the good old way, more people could worship the Lord. Or if we just played the song in the right key, then people could truly worship the

Lord. Or if we just played the music a little quieter, or a little louder, or without drums, or with a choir, or without a choir, or if we would just play some newer songs, or if we would wear slacks instead of jeans, or jeans instead of slacks then people would really worship the Lord. Really? Really? Of course, the point of this is not to re-mitigate the worship wars of the late twentieth century, but rather to illustrate how set in our own cultures we are. So set, in fact, that we allege that unless submission to our personal cultures is reached, people will not be able to worship Jesus. To be sure, our different cultures are good, and certainly, a person or people who are entering into a different culture must change in some ways (for example, Americans visiting the United Kingdom should probably drive on the left side of the road instead of the right side of the road, don't you think?), but those cultures can become counterproductive and even an obstacle when our personal church cultures are held as benchmarks for belonging.

It is true that everyone who follows Jesus will pay a cost, and that cost will be their very lives. In some cases, people pay with their lives because they are killed for their faith. In other cases, people pay with their lives in that they die unto themselves—that is, give up their rights for their ways in exchange for inheriting the right and the freedom to live God's way (and remember, God gave His life for us to be able to live for Him in the first place). Since Jesus already set the cost of following Him, why is that the church today seems to want to add to that cost, and in so doing place an undue burden on some who wish to follow Him? Think about this: it is easier to receive salvation in Jesus Christ than it is to become a member at some churches. Jesus was clear that if a person believes on Him, that that person is saved, and that their lives will now be changed from the inside out as the indwelling Holy Spirit works within them over the course of their life. Yet to become a member of particular church, there are, in some cases, criteria to be met that Jesus Himself did not ask for from His people.

In Matthew 23, Jesus is rebuking the Pharisees for their hypocrisy. At the center of His rebuke is the idea that the Pharisees are demanding that people conform to their manmade culture instead of helping people enter into Christ culture.

Matthew 23:13–22 (NIV 2011) reads:

"Woe to you, teachers of the law and Pharisees, you hypocrites! You shut the door of the kingdom of heaven in people's faces. You yourselves do not enter, nor will you let those enter who are trying to. Woe to you, teachers of the law and Pharisees, you hypocrites! You travel over land and sea to win a single convert, and when you have succeeded, you make them twice as much a child of hell as you are. Woe to you, blind guides! You say, 'If anyone swears by the temple, it means nothing; but anyone who swears by the gold of the temple is bound by that oath.' You blind fools! Which is greater: the gold, or the temple that makes the gold sacred? You also say, 'If anyone swears by the altar, it means nothing; but anyone who swears by the gift on the altar is bound by that oath.' You blind men! Which is greater: the gift, or the altar that makes the gift sacred? Therefore, anyone who swears by the altar swears by it and by everything on it. And anyone who swears by the temple swears by it and by the one who dwells in it. And anyone who swears by heaven swears by God's throne and by the one who sits on it."

What Jesus is saying is that the Pharisees' missionary efforts were producing the wrong results, and it was the results that Jesus was rebuking, not the efforts.[9] The Pharisees were more interested in winning people to their views and positions than they were in winning people to Christ, and this was Jesus's main objection at this juncture.[10] Furthermore, when Jesus makes reference to the gold and the temple, and the altar sacrifices, He is pointing out that the Pharisees were demanding that people use their (the Pharisees) preferred, or favored,

---

[9] Carson, D. A. (1984). Matthew. In F. E. Gaebelein (Ed.), *The Expositor's Bible Commentary: Matthew, Mark, Luke* (Vol. 8). Grand Rapids, MI: Zondervan Publishing House.
[10] Ibid.

methods of worship, and that it is not the method that makes the worship sacred, rather, it is the one to whom the worship is given. If Jesus were to say this today, He might say something like, "You say, 'only music written by Chris Tomlin is worshipful.' Is it the human author of the song that makes the song sacred, or is it the one upon whom the song is centered that makes it sacred?"

If we, as the church, are to indeed live in Christ culture, Christ must be alive and at work in us to such a degree that we lay down our old cultures for His new culture, and that we do not require others to pay extra to take up our culture when Christ's offer is already paid for by Him and offered freely to us. It is impossible for us (the church) to seek after those who do not know the Lord and expect that they will be exactly like us when we find them (I am quite sure that the opposite will be true) because when we find the lost (lost means unsaved, does not yet trust in Jesus), they are just that, lost, and people who are lost do not talk like, walk like, or look like people who are found (found means saved, trusts in Jesus for salvation). And the fact that they are lost does not mean that they are less of a person, or are of less value, than one who is found since everyone is lost at one time or another before they are found, and we (the church) need to remember that.

The kingdom of God is made up of people from every nation on earth, past, present, and future. This means that if we are to be effective ambassadors in our cities, communities, and neighborhoods, it is not enough for us to only seek those who already talk like us, walk like us, and look like us. God's kingdom is bigger than us, and He has room for more people than just copies of ourselves. Our aim, as a royal priesthood (1 Peter 2:9), is not for people to talk like us, but for people (including ourselves) to talk like Jesus. Our aim is not for people to walk like us, but to walk like Jesus. And our aim is not for people to look like us, but for people to look like Jesus. Only in Christ can people from all nations become one nation. Only in Christ can people from all walks of life walk in the light of life together.

In the beginning, humankind was intended by God to live together as more than one nation under God, but as one nation with God, and as one nation in God. And it is to that God, through Jesus Christ is restoring us. Now that we have seen what God has intended for us, let's look briefly at what happened when the human race began to fragment, and the pivotal moments in history that divided the human race along cultural lines.

CHAPTER 3

THE SPIRITUAL ROOTS OF THE CULTURE WARS

> The hardest thing I had to overcome in life? I think racism [sic]. That's so difficult because I don't think anyone can ever understand it. It's [sic] not that people don't want to understand it, but they don't want to touch it.[11]
>
> —Former NFL player Herschel Walker

One of the factors at the heart of human divisiveness is our own personal cultures. We all have personal cultures. We all have traditions we keep, things we enjoy, values we hold, family and friends that we love, the ways we like to worship God (or not worship God, depending on your beliefs, which again is part of your personal culture), ways that we like to have fun, holidays we celebrate, lifestyles we prefer, and so on. Our personal cultures can then be extended to familial cultures and community cultures as we find the types of groups with whom we enjoy being. Culture wars happen when our cultures, whether personal, familial, community, or national, are threatened, or when we perceive our cultures are being threatened.

My (Andrew) oldest son is ten years old (at the time of this writing). He is fifth grade, and later this school year his section on sex education begins. My wife and I homeschool our kids, and we will share the

---

[11] https://www.brainyquote.com/topics/racism_3. Accessed on November 24, 2017 at 9:43pm PST.

teaching load on certain subjects. Our regular homeschool teaching-sharing culture is like this:

My wife: History, reading, math, science, social studies

Me: Pro wrestling, NFL, classic 1980s sitcoms, pizza appreciation, pretend ninja skills

Okay, so my wife is a homeschool teaching champion, and I am, how can I put it, not. But nonetheless, we are approaching this sex education unit, and my wife asks me if I would take the lead and teach that material. Now, both my wife and I are actually having the same kinds of thoughts, which were that we almost wish sex did not exist so that we would not have to teach about it to our kids. How do you answer the questions that will inevitably come up? What about when they ask how *they* themselves were born? To be sure, I did agree to teach the unit (which is still upcoming at the time of this writing), but it does make me a bit uncomfortable. Not because I do not want my son to understand sex in a biblical and responsible way, but because once the topic is breached, it will change him as his understanding of life and how life works will be expanded. And as many parents likely feel, there is a kind of childhood goodness (so to speak) that goes away as they mature.

At any rate, I share that story because the topic of sex, and the sex education unit is threatening the current culture that my wife and I enjoy. But the reality is, that there is no way around it. We have to teach our children about biblical sex, relationships, and the biological truths about their bodies and what happens as they mature. And since this culture change is coming whether we like it or not, the only way we can avoid it is to ignore sex education altogether, or somehow eliminate it from the topics of study, so we do not have to deal with it.

Granted, that is kind of a silly illustration, but the concept is quite similar to our culture wars that we face daily. We have a culture that we like, and that we are used, and then, what we perceive as a threat to that culture reveals itself, and there is no way that we can avoid it, unless we eliminate it. Are you following me in this line of thought? Not only do we treat tough subjects and uncomfortable situations this way, but we also treat people this way. And what's worse, in America we have conflated culture to being equal to, or interchangeable with, skin color. In other words, when we see a person whose skin color is different than our own, we make certain cultural assumptions based on their skin color alone. From there, we determine whether the cultural assumptions we have made are a threat, or potential threat, to our own personal or community culture, and let the divisions begin. It is important to note this at the outset of this and the next chapter because racism is the clearest example of a culture war that we have in America, and it is an example that we can all relate to and understand in some way. This means that, no matter how much we do not want to touch it or talk about it, we have to discuss the problem of racism head on if we are to advance our conversation to the application of Christ culture. So take a deep breath; here we go.

Racism is one of the great divides that exist among humanity. It is a staggering and baffling reality that, no matter how humankind has strived to eradicate it, racism remains in every culture, and in every nation the world over. Perhaps one reason that humanity's attempts to bring an end to such a cultural evil is because, for the most part, humankind has failed to recognize the true roots of racism, thereby only affecting its symptoms instead of its source. Throughout history, humanity has waged the most violent and terrible wars over the trial of racism. Laws have been both enacted and repealed surrounding the problem of racism. Nations have risen to be beacons of equality, only to find themselves (seemingly) hopelessly locked in a catch-22 of racism as its (racism's) intensity increases and decreases over and over from generation to generation. As has been stated previously in this book, here is the crux at the heart of racism:

Once again, racism is not a skin problem; racism is a sin problem.

The sad truth is that as long as people reject Christ's truth concerning humanity, they will also reject His culture, and prejudices of all kinds will continue. To be sure, when I say that people reject Christ's truth concerning humanity, I am including Christians among that group. It is, of course, not my intention to point a blaming or critical finger at anyone, but it is important that we, Christians, do not exempt ourselves from being vulnerable certain kinds of temptation and/or pride. It is absolutely possible that a person can trust Jesus for salvation, and yet still reject other aspects of Christ's truth.

In fact, every Christian takes on that very battle as they journey with Christ. The thing that makes the difference in the life of a believer is whether they allow the Holy Spirit to renew their minds (Romans 12:1–2) so that they can learn to see things through the prism of biblical truth instead of personal pragmatism and preferential justice.

To get closer to the source of racism so it can be effectively addressed, we need to ask a series of basic questions. First, we need to determine what exactly qualifies as a "race" from a biological perspective. Once we know what a race is, we then need to determine what would differentiate one race from another, and this will bring us to an examination of what skin color truly is and whether or not skin color alone can be enough of a factor to conclude that people of different colors are necessarily of different races. Last, we need to look at when "races" actually began. When was it that the one nation that God intended became many nations, and why did that happen?

What Is a Race?

Pay attention right here because the sentence you are about to read is one of the most important sentences in this entire piece of writing: biologically speaking, there is no such thing as differing races among human beings.[12] Let me express that once again: biologically speaking, there is no such thing as differing races among human beings. Why is that such an important sentence? Because it tells us that the biological scientific perspective completely agrees with God's account of creation and of nations throughout scripture. This means that God did not create a multitude of races; He created one race, the human race, and He intended for them to live together, enjoying each other, enjoying creation, and giving glory to the Creator. It perhaps cannot be overstated that if the church today is going to effectively live out Christ culture, then we must see people and treat people in the way that God intended in the first place. And what's more, biological science backs up what God has revealed to humanity about His intentions for them.

[12] Nicki Lisa Cole, The Sociological Definition of Race, https://www.thoughtco.com/race-definition-3026508. Accessed on January 8, 2018.

Unfortunately, with many churches and church leaders, outreach is practiced as though a race is something that God created or intended, when in fact just the opposite is true. The resulting problem here is that now the church is relating to people who are different than them according to a set of standards that are not accurate spiritually, scripturally, or scientifically. It is then not a surprise that the majority of church outreaches within America that attempt to break down racial barriers end up flat and ineffective. Why is this? Because the church is not dealing in reality with respect to race and is therefore not effective in truly showing a person who they are in Christ with respect to so-called racial identity.

Biblically speaking, there are two kinds of classifications given to animate creation at the point of creation. First, in the animal kingdom, there are classifications of *kind*. The creation account in Genesis 1 and 2 shows that the different animals were organized and named according to their kind, and they were to have (and would have) offspring according to their kind. Second, concerning human beings, the distinction was in terms of gender, not race. And that there was a gender distinction did not, and does not, mean that there is or was a different value placed on one gender or another (Galatians 3:28), a point that will be addressed in detail later in this book. The next, and only other, way that people were divided into classifications was at the Tower of Babel, wherein one nation of people were split into many nations. Once more, the different nations did not come with an assignment of value, whether lesser or greater than other nations (Galatians 3:28), yet the physical distinctions between peoples (i.e. languages, traditions, etc.) would now be vastly multiplied, which, the Bible tells us, did make it difficult for people to work together. But here again, this was not one race divided into many races. Even though there are many nations of peoples, there is still only one race of people.

Okay, So Really, What Is a Race?

Inasmuch as humankind has been able to determine, race, as it were, is nearly impossible to define. Since race lacks a biological foundation, race must be determined by other social factors. As a result, everything from skin color, to economic status, to nationality, to regional traditions and customs can be determining criteria in defining one's "race," so it depends greatly upon the ones who doing the defining to come to classification of race. Again, I have to go back to the Bible and make the plea that racial distinctions were never part of God's intention, nor are they supported by biological study, and therefore multiple races among human beings is, at best, a misnomer, and at worst, a gross underestimation and false classification of humanity.

The tragic irony of race is that, while it cannot be defined (because it was not established by God in the first place), race has had innumerable effects on humankind through the ages. And what's worse, the effects of race on humanity have only served to divide people, whether it has to do with the law of the land, or whether it is because people self-segregate themselves, this uncreated and undefinable phenomenon called race has led to very real, and often tragically deadly consequences. In short, racism is one form of discrimination based on differing human distinctives. As with many problems that have ailed the world for millennia, it helps to at least briefly examine where the roots of racism began so that we can better trace its path into American life today.

The Sad Beginnings of Racial Division

Since racism is not a skin problem, rather, it's a sin problem, we can actually trace the foundational roots of racism back to the garden of Eden. To be sure, there were no "races" in Eden. Remember, God did not create, nor intend for there to be, a human racial distinction. Nevertheless, the seeds of sin that give way to depraved out-workings such as racism were certainly in play.

Now, bear with us because we have to go around the block a couple of times to lay out the facts we need to know to best understand where racism comes from. Here we go.

Consider this. There are two essential mind-sets that must be manifested for a given temptation to work well enough that a person will in fact sin. First, the person must be invited to doubt what God has already revealed about Himself and His truth.[13] Of course, because of sin's exponentially damaging effect on humanity, sinning is a pretty easy thing for people to do, and theologically speaking, sin is the default position of humankind. With that said, we do struggle with knowing how to make the right choices, and sometimes even how to tell what that right choice might be. This is where the idea of invitation comes in. To be most effective, sin must invite us to doubt that what God said is actually what He meant. This is why Satan asked Eve if God *really* said that she and Adam would die if they ate the fruit of the tree of the knowledge of good and evil (Genesis 3). Satan had to plant a seed of doubt toward God and what He meant. Now, God is a straightforward being, and He says what He means, so certainly, God meant it when He said that Adam and Eve would die if they ate the fruit, but humankind's ability to rationalize, theorize, and ultimately convince him/herself of all kinds of things, when coupled with doubt, usually leads a person to the next mind-set that gives birth to sin: denying God.[14]

If I believe that God really does not mean what He says when He says it, then I will deny the truth of what He said to justify whatever it is I am about to do (or not do), and this is exactly what Adam and Eve did. They doubted God's intention, then denied His truth and ultimately would sin by eating the fruit, thus ushering sin and death into the world, and into every human being who was not Jesus Christ from that point forward. The Bible teaches us that sin now darkens every human heart, and the book of James tells us that a person's sinful ideas can arise from the evil intentions of their own heart. So in asserting that racism is a sin issue, we connect such sin with the attitudes of our hearts, and the problem is that our hearts come with a presupposed bent toward sin and destruction as opposed to innocence and love.

Does that mean that people are born racist? No, not necessarily, but it does mean that people are born sinful and in need of salvation from and by Jesus Christ. Yet different people will battle different kinds of sin in their lives. For some, racial prejudice may be a serious problem. For others it could be addiction of one kind or another. Still

---

[13] John J. Davis, *Paradise to Prison: Studies in Genesis*, Sheffield Publishing; Salem, WI, 1998, 88–89.
[14] Ibid.

for others it could be something else. Being born with a sin nature does not mean I will fall prey to every kind of temptation and commit every sin imaginable, but it does mean that my default position is going to be one that is contrary to God's will and intentions for my life, and life in general. And whenever we are living contrary to God's intentions and will, we are living apart from faith in Him, and as such, living in sin.

When I think about my life and my childhood, I have all kinds of memories. I can remember the park next door to my grandparents' house that I used to go to play when I was a little boy. I remember going to baseball games, and trying out for Little League when I was eleven years old (my baseball career really stalled once I turned twelve). I remember various friends that I had over the years, holidays, Sunday family lunches after church, and on and on. But you know, I have no memory of my mom teaching me how to lie, how to steal, or how to manipulate people, how to be selfish, or how to hide my actions when I do something that I know is wrong. Nope. All that stuff I learned on my own, and I would bet that you learned most of that stuff on your own too. It's like I was hardwired for that kind of living, and according to the Bible, I am, and so are you. So when it comes to God's revealed word, it is my pre-programmed (that is, pre-programmed by sin) position to doubt God and deny Him and His truths. This of course makes it all the easier for me to be seduced by temptation into sin, and it makes all the easier for me to harbor sinful attitudes in my heart.

People do not like to think of themselves as wicked and evil by default. We do not like to admit how selfish we are, and how much we want everyone else to just get out of our way and let us do whatever we want to do. We do not like to admit that we like to sin, that sinning is fun, and we would rather not stop. And we do not like to admit that there are people that we absolutely hate, for whatever reason, and people whom we feel are beneath us and should be cast aside. We do not like to admit those things, but they are true for every human being, but for the intervention and transformation that happens when one trusts in Jesus Christ. But is it not a compelling thought to think that just as Satan put the seed of doubt into Eve's mind, that such doubting of God's truth might be affecting our ability to acknowledge such things about ourselves? And could not such doubting of God's truth lead us to denying His truth about ourselves, and by extension about each other? Could this have something to do with why problems like racism cannot be extinguished because the problem is not in man's laws but in man's heart?

The book of James 1:13–15 (NIV 2011) puts it this way:

When tempted, no one should say, "God is tempting me." For God cannot be tempted by evil, nor does he tempt anyone; but each person is tempted when they are dragged away by their own evil desire and enticed. Then, after desire has conceived, it gives birth to sin; and sin, when it is full-grown, gives birth to death.

Notice how James says that we are dragged away and enticed by *our own sinful desires*. ***Our own*** *sinful desires*. In other words, our own hearts come up with ways to sin all by themselves, and we listen to our hearts, and then give in to the temptation and sin. Whether the sin is something we do in moment, or an attitude we have that governs our lives, the birth of sin is our own hearts.

Jeremiah 17:9 says that the human heart is "desperately wicked," and "deceitful above all things," and goes on to say in verse 10 that no human being can truly know the motives of their own hearts, but God does. So if the heart is desperately wicked and deceitful above all things, meaning before my heart is loving it is deceitful, and before my heart is generous it is deceitful, and if it is true that my heart then overflows with all kinds of ways to be selfish and sinful, then the sin that I commit against my fellow man is not a corporate institutional problem from somewhere out there. Rather, it's an internal problem in me.

It is important to note that when Adam and Eve were tempted, they were in their sinless state, so sin had to come and present itself to them (i.e., the serpent). However, once Adam and Eve allowed sin into the world, the Bible also says that sin entered the hearts of every human being from then on, and as a result, sin does not need to come in the form of a serpent to tempt us. Our own hearts will do the job just fine. In contrast, one of the evidences that tells us that Jesus is the sinless

Savior and the Son of God is the fact that, just like in the garden of Eden, Satan had to approach Jesus and tempt Him. This time, however, Jesus would resist temptation whereas Adam and Eve did not. Jesus did not have a sin nature passed on to Him from an earthly father as God was/is His father, and this makes the fact of the Virgin Birth all the more important as well (if Jesus had been born of Joseph, Joseph would have passed a sin nature along to Him. God knew this, and thusly called Mary to carry His Son, Jesus Christ, thereby making the way for Jesus to be born sinless).

This is what makes it so critical that we, the church, strive and plea to God that we can be empowered and obedient to live in Christ culture as collective bodies of believers. Without Christ, all we have to tell us how to relate to other people is our own desperately wicked, deceitful, and sin-idea-spewing heart. Let's apply some common sense at this point.

How well will we relate to those who might be different from us if we are only listening to our deceitful, wicked hearts?

Do we really believe that we can truly love people, and accept and welcome them, without following Christ?

The seeds of doubt and denial that have led to racism today were planted in the hearts of humankind in the garden of Eden thousands of years ago. We doubt that God created only one race, and we deny His truth that we were meant to live together, enjoying His presence, and the presence of each other forever. We doubt that God created only one race, and then we deny that all people are of equal and intrinsic God-given value. Furthermore, we doubt that God created only one race, and we deny that it is for God to judge humanity, on His terms, and so we set out to pronounce a verdict for humanity, and when we do, we inevitably come to the conclusion that one race or another must be eliminated. We doubt that God is a fair judge of humanity, and so we deny Him the space to do so (speaking from a human perspective), conveniently forgetting that God judged sin by paying the price for sin Himself in the person of Jesus Christ, so that we, who are the ones with the automatic sinful hearts, could be saved by our faith in Christ as Savior.

And it is when deny that God is the good and just judge that we pronounce death sentences and lives of slavery and indentured servitude upon each other. In short, the seeds of doubt and denial of God will lead people to enslave each other out of the wickedness of their hearts. But the seeds of truth that God has given us through His Word lead to freedom, equality, and true justice for all who will believe on Him.

With an increased understanding of racism's spiritual roots, we can now turn to a brief survey of the progression of racism through centuries, and perhaps have a greater understanding of why Americans view race and racial relations in the ways that we do. We need to better understand the genesis of the pre-conceived ideas that we may have held our whole lives without being fully aware simply because of our cultural conditioning. We need to recognize where we integrate faulty thinking and/or misunderstandings of history and culture in to our everyday lives, and then we can begin to be the people that God intended us to be in the first place.

At the beginning of this chapter, we included a quote from legendary NFL running back Herschel Walker in which he asserted that it is not that people do not want to talk about race; it's that people do not want to touch the subject in the first place. I suggest to you that one of the reasons why we do not want to touch it in the first place is because we know that if we investigate where the hate in our world comes from, we will end up staring at ourselves in our own mirrors, and that is far too horrifying to realize. And I understand. I hate the fact that, apart from Christ, I would be an oppressor of people. Sure, it might not be oppression on the basis of skin color in my case, but it would be some other preference. I do not like to, nor do I want to admit that, but for Christ, I am a wretched individual. Such a thought leaves me feeling helpless and hopeless, but I suppose, without Christ, we *are* without help and hope, aren't we?

But because of Christ, there is help and hope. There is forgiveness, there is transformation on emotional, mental, and spiritual levels (which extend to the practical), there is healing, there is love, there is mercy, and there is life. And like it is with any process of healing and renewal, we need to be honest about the roots and progression of what ails us if we are to effectively overcome in and through Christ. Just like when we go to a doctor because of strange pain we might be feeling, the doctor cannot help us if we are not completely transparent and honest with him/her about when the pain started, what we were doing, and so forth. The truth about humanity and sin's effects on humanity are ugly and terrible, but the truth about who we can be if we would turn to Christ is beautiful beyond measure.

CHAPTER 4

RACISM'S RISE IN AMERICA: HOW THE DOUBT AND DENIAL OF GOD'S WORD HAS SHAPED THE AMERICAN UNDERSTANDING OF RACE

Racism is man's greatest threat to man—the maximum of hatred for a minimum of reason.

—Abraham Joshua Heschel

One of the most common objections to the very existence of God (let alone His motives and intentions toward and for humankind) stems from the idea that, if God was such a good god, He would flip a supernatural switch and take the racism out of everyone (or whatever social/global plague that may be the topic at hand). Yet what God never gets credit for is the fact that He did create a world wherein racism (and for that matter, war, death, starvation, poverty, etc.) did not exist. The problem was that humankind screwed up the plan. To be sure, while God did ultimately defeat sin through the cross and His death and resurrection, thus paying the penalty for sin, He did not remove the temporal consequences of humanity's sin, and it is precisely these consequences that we experience today, one of which is racism.

Another of God's intentions from creation was for humankind to populate the earth and spread across the whole earth. However, from the early chapters in the book of Genesis, we learn that humanity was not about to scatter abroad. Rather, they wanted to band together to prevent such a scattering from happening at all (Genesis 11:4). The account in Genesis then shows us that God was not upset that the people were building a city but that they were disobeying God's command to fill the whole earth and trying to insulate themselves from God's direction and discipline. As is the case when humans doubt and ultimately deny God's truth in their lives, God confounded their plans by confusing the people's language (until this point, everyone on earth spoke the same language and dialect),[15] which would then cause them to scatter about the earth, in accordance to their new languages.

And thus, the earth became multicultural. A plurality of cultures is consistent with God's intention for humanity, and as the science of linguistics has proven, people who gather together in a particular region will, over time, develop their own dialect and language type.[16] Acts 17:26 says that God had "made of one blood all nations of men for to dwell on all the face of the earth," and this is no small statement, or mere example of theological poetry. In this powerful proclamation, the apostle Paul boldly declares that God did not create different races, and yet at the same time, He wanted for the one race of humanity to become many nations, all of which might praise and honor Him. The idea of nations was not a strict result of sin, because it is highly logical that nations would have necessarily developed even if sin had not entered the world, and had humankind obeyed God's command to be fruitful and multiply and fill the whole earth with people. Inasmuch as God intervenes to protect humankind from self-destruction, He also allows humankind the free will to make choices, and oftentimes those choices are a denial of God's truth and thereby destructive toward people and all of God's creation.

As nations would continue to form and rise and fall over centuries, two kinds of nationalism would develop. There is one kind of nationalism wherein people are proud of their country, respect the nationhood of other countries, and are willing to expand their nations through mutual assimilation of different national cultures. Consider the quote from Emma Lazarus that is written upon the Statue of Liberty: "Give me

---

[15] Ibid., 144.
[16] Ibid., 149.

your tired, your poor, your huddled masses yearning to be free." This is the best reflection of healthy nationalism that can be found on a sin-infected earth. America was to be a land in which all cultures and nations of the world could not only have a place to live the life they chose, but wherein different cultures might be brought together and mutually shared among people. This was to be the culture of America in its inception, and I would submit, it is the kind of national culture that many who call America home would want as well (even if there are differing views as to how to best further this ideal).

Another kind of nationalism would also be nurtured and passed along from generation to generation, but this kind of nationalism was rooted in an ugly pride and vicious hatred. This kind of nationalism meant that one nation looked upon another with contempt, and thereby dismissed all peoples from that "contemptible" nation as the worst of humanity, even in some cases alleging a lack of humanity among those who might be considered a lower/lesser race. Initially, this version of nationalism brought a prejudice between people based on their country of origin, and the color of their skin would soon be mixed into the regrettable fray. Later in this book, we will examine the story of the Good Samaritan, and in that example, it is important to understand that the Samaritans would have been a hated people no matter what color they were. All it took was for a person to be from Samaria at that time. This brand of nationalist thought would see some of its tendencies later extended to and conflated with skin color, and it is at this point in history where Americans, and American Christians especially, need to pay careful attention.

Before I go further, it cannot be stated enough that racism is, at its core, a sinful hatred of people. Whether the basis for said hatred is one's country of origin or the color of one's skin, the hatred is the same, and oftentimes, the result is the same: segregation at best and genocide at the very worst. In America, however, we understand the racial argument and struggle in terms of skin color primarily, and of that understanding, there is one dominant narrative that establishes the framework through which we (Americans) view racism.

The popular narrative, essentially, is this: the white man migrated (perhaps illegally) to America and either forced away, enslaved, or killed those who were native to the new world (pre-colonial America). As the white man established his presence in America, he brought slaves from all around the world (Africa, Japan, China, India, among others) to do the physical labor that he (the white man) did not want to do. Such slaves were treated quite harshly and were not even considered fully human to some slave owners. As time would go on, America would war with itself over the legality and ethics of human slavery, ultimately bringing about the Civil War, which led to the outlawing of slavery in America, but sadly, not the eradication of racism.

With slavery now illegal, the white man preserved his self-perceived high stature by enacting segregation laws. Such laws would place limits and boundaries upon people of color and ensure that a plurality of races could never, and would never, coexist. Segregation and later, the famed Jim Crow laws of the southern United States, would lead to what is remembered and celebrated as the Civil Rights Era in the 1960s. The Civil Rights Era would usher in the end of lawful segregation and see America work to integrate peoples of all colors and nationalities into various contexts (school, workplaces, restaurants, and much more).

While the changing of the laws helped to stem the rising tides of racism in some ways, the laws of the land could not reach into people's hearts, and as lawful segregation ended, self-segregation began. The phenomena of "white flight," which is the nickname for the period of time during which businesses owned by white people fled from predominantly black neighborhoods and communities, ostensibly because of their (the white man's) intolerance for people of color. The white man would take his businesses and his money and settle in suburban neighborhoods, leaving the people of color to scrape for a better life in inner cities, ghettos, barrios, and forgotten neighborhoods.

In short, the white man is not only personally oppressive toward people of color, but is culturally (and some argue even biologically) systemically oppressive toward other people groups. The white man has benefitted for centuries with a privilege that comes to him simply because he is white, while people of color are born with a biological handicap, that being a greater amount of melanin in their skin. White people, according to the Western popular narrative, are predisposed to being racist against people of color, while people of color are victims whose resulting distrust and, in some cases, hatred of white people is justified in view of the great many offenses committed against them over the course of American history.

That is the basic narrative of race relations in America. But what of that narrative is true? Certainly, the unfolding of events from wars, to protests, to shifting economic realities are absolute and undisputed facts. But what about the overarching premise that white people have a built-in advantage in life simply because they have a fairer skin tone? And what about the premise that people of color are specifically disadvantaged because of their skin color? Where do these ideas come from? And why have they been so readily assumed, or passively accepted by so many Americans? The answer may surprise you.

To live with oneself, we must justify our motives and actions somehow, and should we give in to our desire for self-sovereignty at the expense of others, we must justify our prejudice and hatred. This is, of course, to say nothing of the fact that if something needs to be *self*-justified, it more than likely is an unjust cause, motive, and/or action. When it comes to racism then, the way another person looks on the outside becomes the internal, spiritual, emotional, physical, and mental justification for another person to hate them.

The Darwinian Evolution of Prejudice

In 1859, Charles Darwin published what is perhaps his preeminent work, *The Origin of the Species: The Preservation of Favoured Races in the Struggle for Life*. In this book, Darwin posited his famous theory about the evolution of animals in general. This same theory would be attributed to human beings in his 1871 work, *The Descent of Man*. Effectively, Darwin's theories concerning the supposed evolutionary development of human beings did more to normalize and popularize racism than any one person had ever done before.[17]

In his works, Darwin suggested that white people were the furthest people descended from the primates, and as such, we were the most

---

[17] Ken Ham and A. Charles Ware, *One Race One Blood* (Green Forest, AR: Master Books, 2013), 22–23.

highly intelligent and highly evolved. In contrast, those people who had not descended far from primates had the darkest skin tone, and while such people were physically stronger, they were less intelligent, low, savage, and degraded. Darwin theorized that white people descended from chimpanzees (citing the high intelligence of the chimpanzee), that Asian people evolved from orangutans, and that black people evolved from gorillas.[18] And it is here that we find the modern American picture of the races, with whites being privileged, middle-brown people being less advantaged, and black people being the lowest form of evolved life.

Darwin's work, while biologically and factually errant (again, if there is no biological basis for race, how then can there be such a thing as race at all? Not to mention what God has revealed in creation about His being the Creator), has done much to, for lack of a better term, *color* the modern Western view point concerning racial reconciliation, racial equality, and race relations. Darwin put into modern terms a kind of hierarchy of the races, based not on anything tangible (though even a tangible measure would continue to be objectionable, but for the sake of argument), but on the kind of worth that he himself ascribed to said peoples. Darwin had now systematized a rationalization that has been used to justify racism, eugenics (*the engineering of a* population through various population controls. It is important to note that the term "population control" actually means the extinction of unwanted people in society through an assortment of population control techniques, i.e. birth control, abortion, euthanasia, among others), and genocides over the past century and a half. And such racism does not stop at the boundaries of skin color when allowed to fester. We need only remember the horrors of World War II and the genocide of the Jews in Europe to see that Adolf Hitler had taken Darwinian ideas and advanced them, eventually leading to Hitler's crusade to exterminate people of his own color but who he would deem were a part of the "Jewish problem."[19]

---

[18] Ibid.
[19] Ibid., 23.

Darwinian Theory in Modern American Practice

Darwinian theory would also heavily influence the ideas of another person whose work has influenced American race relations in substantial ways: Margaret Sanger. Margaret Sanger is best known in America as the primary founder of Planned Parenthood, and she was a staunch advocate of birth control, and particularly abortion. Sanger believed that birth control was the best way to preserve Western culture because birth control provided a means to protect society from she deemed to be the "less fit" of society.[20] Here again, we see the idea that one race, or nation, is superior than another, and therefore, the superior race is the one that should be propagated in pursuit of an all-pure and perfect race of human. Never mind that Darwin's own natural selection theories would appear themselves to argue against such population manipulation. According to Sanger, the "less fit" consisted of people who she considered "defective," people including but not limited to the disabled, immigrants from Southern Europe, people of Latin heritage, Slavs, Jews, and African Americans.[21] Of course, such views concerning humanity did not originate with Sanger or Darwin, but both have drastically shaped how Americans approach the subject of race relations and even the basic value of human life.

Preceding both Sanger and Darwin in advancing the idea that human value has certain criteria that must be met for said person to be "fit" (or allowed to live, for that matter) was a man named Thomas Malthus. Malthus espoused the view that, "If Western Civilization were to survive, the physically unfit, the materially poor, the spiritually diseased, the racially inferior, and the mentally incompetent" needed to be marginalized, quarantined, and suppressed, if not even eliminated from society altogether.[22] Building on teachings like these, Darwin would popularize the notion that people descended from primates (as opposed to being created by a purposeful Creator God), while Sanger

---

[20] Jerry Bergman, *Birth Control Leader Margaret Sanger: Darwinist, Racist, Eugenist* found on https://creation.com/margaret-sanger-darwinian-eugenicist. Accessed on January 22, 2018.

[21] Ibid.

[22] Ibid.

would attempt to introduce societal engineering through birth control to weed out (so to speak) the lesser races of people.

With the popularization, and even systematizing, of racial boundaries being briefly outlined, in what tangible ways have these theories shaped the American racial viewpoint? First and perhaps foremost, in studying Malthus, Darwin, Sanger, and those who carried on their teachings, one will quickly learn that, in their view, the white person can do no wrong since the white person is the most highly evolved of the human races according to their theories. Even a cursory hearing of the modern American conversation concerning race exposes the fact that Americans have come to accept this very premise. Whether they believe it is accurate or not, this is the dominant premise that sets the context for race relations in America. The problem with accepting this premise (that the white person is the highest, best, and purest form of humanity) is that the premise itself is simply not true. To be sure, while the premise itself is not true, the effects of the premise are very true and very real. Let me illustrate.

Some of you reading this book might remember the movie *Back to the Future II*. Of course, the original, *Back to the Future*, was a hugely popular movie that was released in 1985, and part II came out in 1989. In the original, seventeen-year-old Marty McFly, with the help of his friend and resident crackpot scientist Doc Brown, goes back in time from 1985 to 1955, meets his parents, battles the infamous bully Biff Tannen, and saves his parents' future relationship, and by extension his own existence in the process.

In part II, Marty McFly goes to the future (to the year 2015 to be exact, which, ironically and chronologically, is now in the past) where he rescues his future kids from jail and saves them from Biff's grandson, who is, like his grandfather, a bully. While in 2015, Marty finds a 1980s nostalgia store and purchases a sports almanac, which contains every major sporting result from the year 1950 to the year 2000. Marty buys it on a whim but would later throw it away at the urging of Doc Brown. Well, the big wrinkle is that old man Biff Tannen would find the almanac, steal the book and the time machine, and go back to 1955 and give it to himself so he can make himself rich.

When Doc and Marty return to 1985, they notice that everything has changed. The suburban neighborhoods that originally were filled with nice homes and safe streets have now turned into ghetto and project homes, with an obvious influx of drugs and crime overrunning the streets of the once-safe Hill Valley community. Doc Brown soon figures out that Biff had given the sports almanac to himself in 1955, and thus, the 1985 that Doc and Marty returned to was the original 1985, but a 1985 wherein Biff Tannen is rich, powerful, and married to Marty's mom (Biff murdered Marty's dad so he could marry Marty's mom). And of course, the rest of the movie sees Marty and Doc trying to set things right again.

So what do *Back to the Future II* and the problem of race relations in America have to do with each other? Two words: alternate reality. In *Back to the Future II*, Biff created an alternate universe wherein he was the most powerful man in town, married to the prettiest girl in town, and all he had to do was get rid of Marty McFly's dad. In America, we live in an alternate reality concerning race and race relations. Again, this does not mean that the alternate reality is not really real, and all we have to do to overcome is ignore it. That does not work, and it is not appropriate as so many people have suffered for real because of this alternate reality. Furthermore, it is from the sufferings of this alternate reality that the church needs to respond with truth that is built upon truth, instead of reactions based on a warped and twisted alternate reality.

The alternate reality that we live in as Americans is the one that was popularized and systematized in Western culture through the works of Malthus, Darwin, and Sanger. For example, as I previously mentioned, perhaps the preeminent alternate truth stemming from their teachings is the idea that the white person is highest evolved in all of humanity. The truth is that we must accept that first premise, if the rest of their arguments are to be believed. If we are to believe that a black person has a social and human disability and/or handicap for no other reason that the color of their skin, that skin color is being compared to some other skin color, a skin color that is not "disabled" (i.e., white skin).

One simply cannot draw the conclusions that Malthus, Darwin, and Sanger drew without agreeing first to the idea that the white person is the ideal person, evolutionarily speaking, of course.

Second, the problem with accepting these alternate and faulty premises is that, when we try to address them to make course corrections with respect to how we treat one another, we respond to an alternate theory instead of the truth. When we do that, we've already begun building our racial reconciliation houses on crooked foundations. If we are going to make actual strides in the area of racial reconciliation, we must start from a place of truth, and not from the alternate reality theories put forth by some of the most rabid racists who have ever breathed oxygen on this precious earth.

Think about it. How can people experience equality when equality is something that must be worked for, instead of a place from which we start? Remember back to the creation account in Genesis and recall God's intentions for humankind as we have laid out in this book so far. What is the most essential element of the creation account that is missing from the evolutionary one? The existence of God. God is the one who gives humanity its equality, and God is also the one who established one race of people, not many. God is the one who desired that this one race of people would multiply all over the earth and become many nations, all of whom would respect and honor each other, and revere and celebrate Him.

God is the standard of equality, not humankind. Yet with God removed from creation and His intentions forgotten, humankind must strive for equality alone, with no objective standard for said equality. At that point, man begins to look at physical characteristics and cultural tendencies to determine just what the proper standard might be. Ultimately, people crown themselves king of the world, and their standards of equality are really inverted reflections of their own hatred and malice toward others. And make no mistake, Christians and non-Christians alike are susceptible to this kind of downward spiral thinking.

Third, as has been written in an earlier chapter, racism is the fruit born of the doubting of God, and the denial of His truth, and to fully deny God's truth, one must deny His existence. If God does exist, and He did reveal Himself to humanity, and if He is trustworthy, then His truth, whether acknowledged or not, cannot be denied as long as He exists. As a result, those who are consumed with hatred and prejudice will find ways to (seemingly) erase God from existence and put forth an evolution of man wherein "be fruitful and multiply" is exchanged for population controls, and the horrible mistreatment and slaughter of all those not deemed worthy to live.

With God eliminated from creation, as the evolutionary worldview asserts, the goals of said worldview become precisely the opposite of God's intentions for humanity. Instead of being fruitful and multiplying to fill the earth, our alternate reality says to abort, end, isolate, or otherwise dismiss all life that is not convenient to the stated, preferred, and desired lifestyle that comes from the evolutionary worldview. Instead of equality being given to all people by God, equality is earned only when a person meets certain predetermined criteria.

Instead of the color of our skin being an outward manifestation of the astounding and boundless creativity of God, the color of our skin is the outward manifestation of the level of our human value. Instead of people seeing people as God intended them to be, we see each other as the caricatures that are portrayed through the awful narrative that our current alternate reality has produced. In America's alternate racial reality, we do not live together so much as we try to outlive each other, all the while praying that those we personally find undesirable might be rid from our midst.

The influence of evolutionary theory and discriminatory exclusive thought has darkened the skies of freedom and equality in America since before its founding. The fertile ground of American soil cries out with the blood of untold and unheard of martyrs who have lost their lives for nothing more than the color of their skin. And as the truth that all people are created equal by God is undeniable, the depravity of the hearts of people, and the promotion of the atmosphere of white superiority (which again, finds its popular roots in Darwin's theory of evolution) continue to frame the American relational culture between ethnic groups.

All told, there is no question that America's great history is also marred with the stains of racism throughout its lifespan, and even leading up to today. It is not a surprise that a culture who bases their treatment of each other on false and godless premises would then try to remedy said problems with God. To be sure, overturning hateful, prejudiced, and racist laws was absolutely necessary for America, but overturning a hateful law does not, unfortunately, overcome a hateful heart.

And that brings us to the question of how can relational divisions like racism be defeated? What role does the church have to play in seeking justice for God's beloved creation? Inasmuch as we have begun to see where our American views of racism have developed, it is equally as important to note the approaches to deal with racism that, while successful to certain degrees, are ultimately powerless against the spiritual roots of racism. As we survey our human attempts to combat prejudice, we will begin to see just how unique and critically essential of a role the church can play in seeking justice for humankind, and in breaking the spiritual chains of discriminatory bondage that plague humanity as a whole.

CHAPTER 5

RACIAL SEDATIVES

The best way to stop discrimination on the basis of race
is to stop discriminating on the basis of race.

—John Roberts

I (Andrew) am mixed ethnically. My mother is white, and my biological father was black/ (I never knew my biological father, which is why I refer to him in distant terms.) My biological father's name was Charles. Charles was born in 1950 in Coldwater, Mississippi, in the heart of the South, and in the midst of Jim Crow segregation. When Charles grew to be a little boy, my grandparents moved from Coldwater, Mississippi, to Memphis, Tennessee. My grandfather, Sam, would take his young son, Charles, to get ice cream at a general store in Memphis every now and then. Sam and Charles were not allowed to go into the store. Instead, they had to go around to the back of the store, where the store manager would serve them from a small, walk-up window. From the way that my aunt (Charles's sister) recalls the story, I am sure that, at the time, Charles was glad to have ice cream. I mean, almost every kid loves an ice cream cone. But for Sam, the experience was bittersweet at best because Sam knew that one day Charles would ask why they were never able to go inside and sit down in the store to eat their ice cream, and when Charles would ask that question, Sam would have to say, "It's because our skin is black."

My aunt also reminds me of the days when the Memphis Zoo only allowed black people into the zoo on Thursdays (this policy was dissolved, after a series of protests, on December 1, 1960). The Memphis

Zoo would literally put out a sign that said that no white would be allowed in the zoo on that day (Thursdays). Thursdays at the Memphis Zoo were also garbage collection days, and one would suspect that it is doubtful that such an alignment was pure coincidence. I have five children of my own, and even the thought of having to look them in the eyes and tell them that through no fault of their own, because of a quality of their being that was completely out of their control, they were not allowed to do this or that. It is a heartbreaking thought, but it was reality for people of color in America for generation after generation.

As America grew, and Western culture changed, to the credit of the United States, the abhorrent practice of race-based slavery was outlawed. Yet while the law of the land would indicate a change in people's perceptions of one another, the inward relational malice that hid inside many Americans still remained. Even after the Emancipation Proclamation, America still needed to move on such basic matters as the right to vote (for people of color and for women), the right to own property (again, for people of color and for women in general), along with matters of legal ethnically mixed marriages, rights to quality education, and so much more.

This cultural stalemate led to America's adopting of segregation laws, or the fallacious idea of "separate but equal." With slavery, segregation laws were essentially a given. Since the lower members of society (i.e., slaves) were considered property and not actually people, they did not have the freedom to move about the neighborhoods and towns, and it was easy to keep the "less fit," as some would suggest, in check.

However, with the end of slavery in America came a new problem: How does a society whose primary leaders do not want to be ethnically integrated live in a lawfully forced environment of ethnic integration? The answer? Well, to society at the time, the answer was the aforementioned Jim Crow laws.

Now, remember how we learned earlier that racism's popular roots can be traced back to Charles Darwin and Margaret Sanger? The Jim Crow laws of the south (1877–1960s) represent the furthering of the views of Darwin and Sanger. Check this out.

Charles Darwin advanced the theory that God had nothing to

do with the creation of people, and that people evolved over time into different races, whose value and worth could be discerned based on the color of their skin, with the purity scale ranging from white (most pure) to darkest brown (the least pure). Margaret Sanger then expanded that idea to include all those that she believed were "less fit" in society (as mentioned, the disabled, the handicapped, in addition to the aforementioned racial distinctives). One of Sanger's greatest fears was that the "less fit" would continue to procreate and ultimately take over civilization. So Sanger became an enthusiastic supporter of birth controls and aborticides (pills that terminate a pregnancy within days of a woman becoming pregnant). Sanger's ultimate goal was to produce and preserve a superior race, and she began taking physical steps to that end when she opened up her first birth control center in a poor neighborhood in Brooklyn in 1916.[23] Sanger would expand her birth control centers into specifically "colored" and poor cities and towns throughout the northeastern United States. Margaret Sanger was convinced that if the superior white race was to be preserved, the lesser races, whom Sanger termed *dysgenic*, would need to be firmly contained, if not erased from America entirely. Sanger even employed black ministers, doctors, and social workers to gain the trust of the black community so that they might, through Sanger's "population controls," be stopped from "over-breeding" and threatening white supremacy in America.[24]

From here, take that summary of information and examine the Jim Crow laws of the southern United States, particularly those that were prominent in the 1900s. Here are a few examples:

a. A black male was not to extend his hand to shake a white male's hand because it implied that the two were socially equal.
b. A black male was not to offer any part of his body to a white female, or he could be charged with rape.
c. Blacks and whites were not to eat together, and if they did, they had to have a partition between them.

---

[23] Ibid.
[24] Ibid.

d. White drivers had the right of way at all intersections, and at all times[25]

The prevailing fear at the time was the "mongrelizing"[26] of the white race, whereby so-called inferior races would intermarry and/or have children with white women, which would irreversibly cripple the social dominance of the white race. The only answer, according to many whites at the time, was rigid racial segregation. Does not this kind of mind-set carry with it the inhumane stench of the teachings of Darwinism and Sanger? Having come through so much ethnic division and hatred, it is no wonder that there remains to this day a distrust between ethnic groups in some instances. America has been the home of a virtual kaleidoscope of ethnicities since her beginnings, and yet America's citizens and immigrants are still learning how to live together. And to think, all this is because people continue to doubt and deny the one true God and His truths about who we are as a people.

Lawful segregation was a way to appease those who did not affirm the basic, essential, and intrinsic equality of all human beings. Lawful segregation was a way to justify one culture's hatred of another and a way to ensure that the "threatening" culture would never overwhelm the "good" culture. In many ways, segregation was a kind of "lateral move" in America's ethnic relational history. I say "lateral" because, while the abolition of slavery was a tremendous move forward, segregation did nothing to solve the underlying issues of hatred that give birth to prejudices of all kinds in the first place. In fact, one might argue that our efforts to become united through our diversity after legalized segregation have actually prolonged the racial divide in America.

Right now, you might be thinking, *Well, duh! Of course! Segregation prolonged racial division. The very definition of segregation is racial division.* And you are correct. But segregation is not just a matter of law. One of the worst things that segregation did was to teach all people how to keep themselves divided. Segregation taught Americans how to draw cultural lines in the proverbial sand so that their own personal cultures might

[25] https://ferris.edu/HTMLS/news/jimcrow/what/. Accessed on January 24, 2018.
[26] Ibid.

not be threatened, or even shared, for that matter. As the Jim Crow laws were overturned, and as the Civil Rights era brought another measure of equality to Americans, our nation was once again faced with the challenge of learning to live with each other and learning how to love one another. Unfortunately, we, as a people, in an effort to bridge our divides, ended up self-segregating ourselves, which while a self-imposed boundary, is not immediately or on the surface objectionable, still leaves Americans divided and virtually in the same place we've been since the Civil Rights Era of the 1960s. And it is these self-imposed boundaries, usually implemented in an effort to find unity, that are ultimately only sedatives that ease some immediate pain, but come up woefully short in solving the problem.

Trying to Get Used to the Pain but Not Actually Dealing with It

A sedative is a medication that one can take that alleviates the immediate pain one might be feeling at the moment. The shortcomings of a sedative are obvious in that, while there might be immediate pain relief, said pain relief is only temporary, and the underlying cause of the pain has not been dealt with at all. A racial sedative, then (as we echo this chapter's title), is a measure of support to help alleviate ethnic relational pain that does have a small degree of effect, but that does not address the root issues of division. As a nation, we've become very good at doling out racial sedatives to make ourselves feel better for the relational sins we have committed against each other.

For example, consider the work/education program, Affirmative Action. Affirmative Action was originally enacted in 1961 by then-President John F. Kennedy, and it was aimed largely at a discriminatory workforce. At the time, segregation was still the law of the land in many states, and as such, the federal government took steps to promote better access to employment for people of color and/or people from poorer economic areas. Affirmative Action was certainly a noble step from America's leaders, and there are many people who have benefitted from the program, bettering their lives as a result. However, objectively speaking, Affirmative Action and movements like it, while they may increase diversity on a hiring roster, do not increase diversity of community and/or relationship among people. Nor can such programs deal with hateful prejudices at its source, which, as we have hopefully made abundantly clear, is in the spirit and attitude of the human heart.

Additionally, Affirmative Action comes with some difficult albeit likely unintended consequences. First, Affirmative Action by practice is discriminatory, except in this case, the discrimination is "reversed" from jobs or spots in school open only to whites, to certain jobs and a certain number of student spots only being open to people of color and/or people who are economically disadvantaged. Ethnicity and income are two of the chief factors of record when it comes to Affirmative Action.[27] Here again, I am not putting down the program itself, nor am I blind to some its benefits, but that fact remains that Affirmative Action was a response to ethnic segregation with a different kind of ethnic segregation. Now, instead of segregating out of hate, this kind of segregation is, in theory, seemingly out of sympathy and the pursuit of equality and justice.

And I suppose here, the philosophical questions of "What is equality?" and "What is justice?" might be raised with good reason. Does equality mean that there are proportionate percentages of ethnicities represented in every workplace and schoolhouse across the nation? Is equality a matter of income, meaning that to be equal everyone must earn the same amount of money? Is equality based on the percentages of ethnicities within a single community being equally represented (in terms of percentage) at work and school? Is equality giving everyone an equal result, or the freedom for everyone to have an equal opportunity? If the premises put forth by Darwin and Sanger are not an accurate picture of humanity, how can we effectively measure equality based on inaccurate assumptions in the first place? And what is justice? Is justice the achievement of equality? And if so, again, what is equality?

Another racial sedative is the Affordable Housing initiatives that have been implemented over the past several decades. In fact, I would

[27] Alia Wong and Isabel Fattal, *The Complicated History of Affirmative Action: A Primer* found on https://www.theatlantic.com/education/archive/2017/08/the-complicated-history-of-affirmative-action-a-primer/535707/. Accessed on January 25, 2018.

argue that a decent portion of the results of the federal Affordable Housing efforts paint a very good picture of the spiritual roots of prejudice. The idea of federal Affordable Housing projects were, on the surface, twofold; first, to provide access and opportunity to purchase a home for the disadvantaged and underprivileged in our communities, and second, to further integrate neighborhoods ethnically. Unfortunately, just like with Affirmative Action, a social initiative might make the surface look better for a little while, but it cannot even attempt to bridge the depth or the width of the human relational chasms that lurk in the hearts of human beings.

On June 28, 1953, a bomb exploded and destroyed a recently purchased house on 430 East Olive Avenue in Memphis, Tennessee. The home had been bought by the Williams family, a black family who would have joined roughly seven other black families in a predominantly white neighborhood.[28] The whites had had enough of the government-prescribed integration and did something about it. This attempt at neighborhood integration preceded the integrations of public schools, restaurants, buses, and a host of other establishments, and until the bomb exploded, it was going "relatively" smoothly.[29]

What the Affordable Housing problems revealed about the spiritual roots of racism was that, ultimately, the battle was over the preservation of one's favored or preferred culture, and if blaming the color of someone's skin would help justify that prejudice, then so be it. As a predominantly white culture began to change, those who were threatened reacted without mercy and in ways void of even the smallest semblance of human compassion and decency. If you are anything like me, you will admit that when things threaten your personal culture, it makes you uncomfortable, and should those threats continue, your first line of defense is to separate yourself from that culture. Should that separation prove unsuccessful, and you remain unwilling to make room to assimilate new aspects to your familiar personal culture, more permanent measure of culture threat removal will likely be employed.

---

[28] Preston Lauderbach, *Memphis Burning* found on https://placesjournal.org/article/memphis-burning/?gclid=EAIaIQobChMIwfiqxdDx2AIVTG5-Ch1L3AnUEAAYASAAEgJSO_D_BwE. Accessed on January 25, 2018.
[29] Ibid.

Certainly, racial (or cultural) sedatives can be used to help mitigate the pain of a threatened personal culture, but unless our hearts are transformed to see people as more than a negative demographic, we will not get any better.

I would also submit that the church has become good at the administration of racial and cultural sedatives as well, which is especially tragic because the church is the one institution that does not need to rely on such placebos to address race relations. And why not? Because the church is the ambassadors of Christ, and the church brings the message of Christ, the Living God, to a lost, divided, and spiritually dead world. The church can combat racial prejudice at its spiritual source, yet, much like popular culture, the church has become too used to the alternate reality put forth by Darwin and Sanger and has become too comfortable in her own self-segregated sanctuaries.

I must acknowledge that I am not surprised at a godless world for trying to right wrongs without God. The godless world does not know God, nor do they believe in Christ, so why would they go to God's word, or rely on His truth, to face matters such as the ones being discussed in this book? And again, America has done what America can do, which is to pass laws to protect the residents of this great land, and to repeal the laws that place Americans in danger of each other. But it is the church's mandated mission to bring the hope of Christ to the lost, as Christ died and rose again to unite His children in Him. The fruit that the Holy Spirit produces has never had, and will never have, any laws that can impede their progress and effects. So why is it that Martin Luther King Jr. is right? Why is Sunday morning in America still the most segregated hour in the nation? How can a people who have the truth of God in their hearts, and in their hands, be okay with such a status quo?

In the introduction to this book, we made the stark claim that the church has abdicated her responsibility in helping to promote justice across ethnic lines. It is, of course, not our intention as the authors of this book to unnecessarily infuriate Christians, nor dismiss the Christians who are on the front lines of battle. Nonetheless, recent Gallup/Lifeway statistics tell us that just over two-thirds (67 percent) of American Christians are already "doing enough" to be ethnically diverse, and less than half (40 percent) of American church-goers believe that their church should be more ethnically diverse.[30] The same study shows that a whopping 86 percent of American churches are comprised predominantly of one ethnic group.[31] To be sure, if the church has not abdicated her responsibility, then should we not see a greater ethnic diversity in the American church from week to week? By the numbers, 8.5 out of every 10 churches in America are made up of one ethnic group, and two-thirds of those said believers are just fine with that. Perhaps ironically, 90 percent of Christians say that racial reconciliation is mandated by God.[32] At what point is the rubber not meeting the road? From these statistics, the church talks as though a commitment to ethnic diversity is commanded of them by God, yet at the same time, an overwhelming majority of the church is content with things as they are, and according to the survey, are not interested in doing much more. If those numbers are indeed an accurate reflection of the mood of the American church at press time, it is hard to see how the church has done anything but abdicate her responsibility in this area. How can the church be so convinced of a God-given command and yet not actually carry it out? In learning some of the answers, we learn of the racial and cultural sedatives that the church has become accustomed to over the past sixty-plus years. It is also important, and admittedly painful, to remember that discrimination is discrimination no matter what context might be cradling the practice. In other words, to select one group of people and administer a special treatment that is different from how others are treated, simply because of the racial makeup of said people, is still discrimination.

Sedative 1—Naïve Ignorance

At the outset, perhaps one of the reasons for this disconnect of Great Commission obedience is that many Christians simply do not recognize

---

[30] Bob Smietana, *Sunday morning in America is still segregated – and that's OK with worshippers*, found on http://lifewayresearch.com/2015/01/15/sunday-morning-in-america-still-segregated-and-thats-ok-with-worshipers/. Accessed on January 25, 2018.

[31] Ibid.

[32] Ibid.

that relational cultural prejudices and racism still exist. After all, that was my (Andrew's) position until relatively recently. I was fine with the status quo because, since I had no problem with different ethnicities personally, I figured that all people, no matter what their ethnicity, would know that they were always welcome around me. But here's the rub with this assumption: I was just assuming that, and I was doing nothing in my life, or in the lives of others, to make that a reality. I was substituting the laws of the land for my obedience to Christ. I figured that since racism is no longer legal, everything should be just fine. I rationalized my apathy by thinking that if people want to come to my church they will, and if not, that's their issue. In other words, if you were in my life, and I had the opportunity to invite you into Christ culture with me, I would neglect to do so and then say that my neglecting to invite you was your fault, and you should have known that you are always welcome. And since you are always welcome, I do not need to actually invite you. The invitation is a standing one and that should count. How wrongheaded is that? It is not other people's fault when it is *we* who do not invite them in the first place. The simple truth is that I was not intentionally trying to bring the peace of Christ to anyone outside of those whom I felt the most comfortable with, culturally speaking. I submit that it is assumptions like this that have played a major part in the church's lack of effectiveness concerning racial and cultural reconciliation over the past 120 years.

Sedative 2—the Outreach Event

From time to time the church is convicted on an area of ministry that may have been lacking in either intentional execution, or actual execution. To a positive end, many churches typically demonstrate a responsive attitude to this kind of correction, and they do want to make a worthwhile difference in their communities. The problem here is not so much with the church as an organization, but with the unintended consequences that can lead to church-goers only practicing outreach on "special event days" and the like, without actually applying outreach as a part of regular life. I suppose such a thing could be described as outreach by association. In other words, it is as if some church-goers say something like, "I go to _____ church. *They* did an outreach to inner city youth; therefore *I* reach out to inner city youth." While it is certainly important to support our churches when special events and outreaches happen, unless our hearts are inclined toward those being reached as a regular part of our lives, it will be difficult to see lasting fruit be produced as a result of these kinds of efforts. Biblical compassion and evangelism cannot only be true on the flyers and posters of our churches, or on only one or two days per year, such attributes must be true of the hearts of individual believers if said attributes are going to be true of our churches.

Sedative 3—Programs, Programs, Programs

As a pastor, I can tell you from direct experience that one of the consistent fallback, go-to ministry moves is the institution of various ministry programs to address specific needs, concerns, and/or areas of spiritual growth. For example, if there are couples going through relationship and marital issues, you'll likely see a marriage small group or a gathering about relationships spring up. Usually these programs come with a workbook (perhaps not unlike the one you are reading right now), group study, etc. The reason programs can become a sedative is because many churches, church leaders, and church-goers can fall into the trap of believing that a program will cure in people's hearts what only Christ can cure. I have yet to hear of someone saying, "I heard that you all read *Purpose Driven Life* fifteen years ago so you all must be on point with purpose. Count me in!" Even something like *Purpose Driven Life* has no purpose unless the reader applies the truths that they read in their lives. To be sure, I would doubt that such a mind-set is the intended one when applying a program to address a spiritual issue in the church, but it can be the result if we are not careful in how we present and teach said information.

Now, the irony is not lost on me that this very book and supplemental materials can constitute a church program. And hopefully, many churches are using this material to shed light on the subject of culture wars and cultural reconciliation among their congregations. At the same time, if you or your church is relying the mere fact that you are reading this book, or going through the group study to be the sole evidence of your church's or your own renewed focus on building cross-cultural relationships, I am afraid that after the excitement wears off, you will be right back where you started, and likely looking for the next program. A program in its proper place can be a great tool to help inspire God's people to action in their communities, but it is important to know that a program is just that, a tool to help as you align yourself (and maybe your church) with God's will in this area.

Sedative 4—Split Services

I want to remind you here that we are talking about cultural reconciliation (there is only one race, but many cultures, both personal and communal). Inasmuch as the topic of this book is about how the church can more effectively reach the different cultures in their communities, churches themselves are also a microcosm of different cultures, and an individual church can learn a lot about how it will fare in reaching different cultures in its community by examining how well it welcomes and embraces differing cultures within its own body of people. For example, there is perhaps no bigger culture war within a church than the music/ worship wars. Having served as a music pastor prior to becoming a teaching pastor, I can tell you that the music departments in many churches likely carry along the nickname the "War Dept."

Granted, music is a very beautiful, powerful, and emotional part of creation. It has been said, and it is likely true, that there are more people who remember the words of their favorite worship songs than who remember the points of their pastor's sermons. And as generations pass, there are renewed, vigorous worship wars within the church. On one hand, you have a people who have served the church faithfully for decades upon decades, who have sung certain anthems of faith during that time, and who do not want those anthems to be forgotten, or even sung differently. On the other hand, new generations bring new expressions of musical worship, and the new generations desire inclusion in primary worship services. However, to include the new songs, it means that older songs are not sung as often. This is a prime example of what we have been talking about concerning real or perceived threats to our preferred cultures. Within the church, in many cases, we see each other as a threat to our preferred cultures of musical worship, and so we fight, oftentimes tooth and nail, to preserve our cultures.

To alleviate the strain, many churches adopt multiple music styles during their morning services. This practice is not necessarily bad in and of itself. I want to be sure to be clear that I believe that God places the leaders He wants in leadership of His people, and I trust that those leaders are leading to the very best of their abilities. At the same time, just like how we try to substitute programs and special events for personal obedience to God's commands for our lives, sometimes our efforts to help quench the tides of relational unrest can have unintended consequences too.

In setting up stylized services to appeal to various demographics, while we are attempting to bridge divides, we run the risk of actually keeping everyone divided. And when our churches stay divided within themselves, they do not learn how to live together and love one another. Now, how are we going to effectively reach outside cultures that are different than us if we cannot embrace and learn to mutually share the different cultures that exist within our own churches? When, in the church, we put this group over here, and that group over there, and this group at this time, that group at that time, and so on, we are practicing a type of self-segregation that may be hindering our obedience to the Great Commission.

To be clear, this section is not advocating a position against split services in totality. What is being suggested is that church leaders need to closely examine and evaluate *why* they have split services. If we are separating our people because they are unwilling to share each other's cultural contributions, and/or because they are threatened by generational or other cultural differences, then it is quite possible that we are enabling people's selfish sin.

Christ culture is a both/and, not an either/or set up. Again, look at what God intended, what God created, and what God commanded to see this. God intended for all people to be able to live together inasmuch as they can share the beautiful earth that God created to fill it with people. To be sure, such a filling would have created multiple cultures, but those cultures were not designed to exist in a sin-fallen environment.

Therefore, it stands to reason that without sin, the cultural divisions we experience today would not be endured. God created a people who could understand each other and who had the capacity to worship Him unfettered by sin (until sin's entrance into the world). And then, even after sin's entrance into the world, Jesus Himself commanded His church to make disciples of all nations. All nations. Every culture. The church can be the one example on earth where everyone has a seat at the table. The church does not have to and should, wherever possible, strive not to create the same kinds of cultural lines and distinctions between people that the world does. Furthermore, if/when we, as the church, enable our people to draw lines between each other based on personal cultural preferences, we are not helping them grow spiritually to learn how to bridge cultural divides.

Think of it this way: Imagine your dining table in the dining room of your house. Maybe you have six chairs surrounding the table. You know what kinds of foods you like to prepare, and everyone in your household has their favorite seats at the table. You usually eat at a certain time, and your pre- and post-meal routines work like a well-oiled machine. What happens when a guest comes over to eat with you? Your whole routine is altered, at least somewhat, if not entirely. Of course, we do not mind entertaining guests and making them feel welcome, we enjoy it. Hospitality is rewarding for all involved, and it is an excellent way to share God's love with others. But what if your one and done meal guest decided to come back every week, and then every week turned into three times a week, and then three times a week turned into every day, and ultimately your dinner guest moved in and never left? It would forever change your meal-time culture, and a permanent change to familiar culture is the kind of change that people have the most difficult time accepting and adapting to. And how much more so when the change is represented in an actual person and not just a worship song or Bible translation.

Perhaps for you, it is outside the realm of actuality that someone could just move in to your house and stay forever, but for the church, God expects that to be a consistent and constant reality. God does not cease to bring His people across the paths of those who are lost. With regularity, those who are lost differ in culture from those who belong to Christ. Are we willing to embrace someone else's culture, and share ours with them on a long-term basis? Or do we really want everyone we meet to ultimately be exactly like us?

Sedative 5—The "Fit in" Dilemma

And now we come to the ultimate social mountain, the high peak of "fitting in." Our whole lives we chase this elusive and mythical goal with the bleak promise that if we can find a place where we can fit in, we'll know we've found our place in life. Yet, how many people actually feel like they fit in anywhere, let alone when they visit a church for the first or second time? Fitting in is a dilemma because there is a truth to the importance of group chemistry within any culture, while at the same time, we often rationalize away a person's absence by saying, "They just did not fit in." In reality, maybe they had a lot to bring to the table, and we were not willing to accept that they operate a bit differently than our expected norms. Of course, team chemistry is a good thing when it is in proper place in social and relational order. For example, workplaces consider how a prospective employee might fit in with their current work culture, and to a degree, this is important. You probably would not want to hire a dentist when you are looking to hire an auto mechanic. But how far should we take the idea of fitting in? Is it not also appropriate to adapt ourselves to new cultures as opportunity arises?

Let's go back to our figurative dining room table for a moment. When someone comes over for dinner once, we have no problem putting out an extra chair for them and setting an extra place for them at the table. If we are having a potluck that evening, we do not mind them bringing a dish to share as well. After all, we are having a friend over, and we want to make a good impression on them so they know how much we care for them and how welcome they are. Again, one day, first-time visitors are just fine. They pose no apparent threat to our personal or community cultures, and we would love it if they came back because it would affirm that we were great hosts the first time around.

It is another matter altogether if the same person were to come to your house with the intention of eating with you every day, and they brought food that they wanted to include among your regular menu items. Of course, putting out an extra chair and eating someone else's food is fine for one day, but for the foreseeable future? What if by eating their food, we do not get to eat our favorite dish as often as we would like? And what about the chairs around the table? It would be much easier if the person could somehow fit in to the chairs that are already there and learn to like the food that we like if this is going to be a long-term thing.

Certainly, we would not normally or outwardly express such discomfort concerning bringing in new people to our church families, but many churches have become comfortable with this kind of approach toward new people in their midst. We love them on the first day, we are glad to see them on the second day, but if they make it a habit to be with us, we want them to fully assimilate into our preestablished ways and forms. And should the new person try to bring a piece of their culture into the mix, such a suggestion is often met with resistance, and in some cases, even hostility.

One of the constant themes in the apostle Paul's letters to the various churches and believers in the New Testament early church period was the idea of Christ culture. Paul was teaching Jews and Gentiles how to love each other and worship God together. This meant that there were some things that both Jews and Gentiles would need to let go of (particularly early pagan practices and legalism), and there were other aspects of their cultures that they were to share with each other. However, Paul was teaching them how to come together and live and worship in Christ culture.

In Christ culture, instead of making a person fit in to a pre-established form, or instead of appeasing people's familiar preferences by separating them into service category demographic types, a place is made for that person to be able to not only share in the cultures of those who preceded them, but also for the person to be able to bring their God-given uniqueness to the table. We have to remember that God intended for the earth to be full of people who have freewill and innovative and creative minds. Think about what the world would be like if there were no sin. Granted, we cannot imagine a world without sin, but if we could, how might our cultures look when they come together? I submit that all of our human cultures were to be under the sovereignty of Christ culture, and under that sovereignty, there is room for all of us to have a seat at the table, for all of us to bring a dish to the dinner, for all of us to bring our songs to the worship service, and for all of us to worship Jesus and follow Him in a unity that is only found in Him.

Jesus comforted His disciples in John 14 with the truth that should He go away, He would prepare a place for each of them in His Father's house, wherein are found many rooms. And Jesus promised that He would take His disciples to be with Himself, so that they could be wherever He was. It is staggering to think that the God of the universe, who saved me from myself and my preference for sin over Him, would not only save me and mature me but prepare a place for me with Him and promise to take me there. And Jesus, is not asking us to fit in. Rather, He wants to be who He created us to be in the first place, and in this life on earth, He, through the work of the indwelling Holy Spirit, matures us as grow in the knowledge and obedience of Him. Each and every one of us was created by God uniquely, beautifully, and wonderfully, on purpose, and for a purpose, and in Christ culture, we all live those truths out together.

In contrast, when we try to get people to conform to our human cultures, this is when all the troubles we have been discussing in this book begin to rear their regrettable heads. Our human cultures are fragile and conditional, and they only work when they are not threatened or replaced. But Christ culture is never threatened, it is not fragile, and it does not depend on surrounding circumstances or protective church and/or social policies for it to remain.

Unity by Way of Human Diversity Is Impossible

In Ephesians 4, the apostle Paul teaches the church about what it means to achieve in unity. In our culture, we believe that unity is the same thing as peace, which we interpret to be the absence of conflict. Furthermore, our culture teaches us that we can be united around our differences, and therefore we are constantly reminded about how different we are from each other, and somehow from that, we are supposed to find common ground. But Paul in Ephesians teaches just the opposite when he says that what and who we unite in and around as people is only Christ Jesus. We are to put off, or do away with, the things that are sinful and destructive, and put on our new selves, which is/are "created after the likeness of God in true righteousness and holiness" (Ephesians 4:24).

In Ephesians 4:14, Paul says that when we are not united in Christ—when we are not surrendered to Him as a people—we are like children tossed about by the waves, and we are vulnerable to all kinds of deceitful teaching and duplicitous schemes.

Missiologist, author, and pastor Ed Stetzer notes, "It's [sic] hard for Christians to say that they are united in Christ when they are congregating separately."[33] Perhaps it is because we, as the American Christian church, are not united in Christ that we go along with what Darwinistic evolutionary theory says about humanity, that we are different races, each with a different intrinsic value and worth, that is displayed through our evolutionary heritage as seen in our resulting skin tones. If that is the case, then it is not any wonder as to why we might be threatened by cultures that are different from our own, especially those different cultures that can be found in our hometowns and local communities.

When we are not united in Christ, we have to find something else to unite around, and that always ends up being our own familiar and comfortable preferences. And when we try to shape or reform others into expressions of our own preferences, we inevitably end up separated by hostility and segregated by choice. But there is hope.

The Christian church in America has an opportunity right now to invite people into Christ culture. Christ culture is not my culture, and it is not your culture. It is Christ's culture, and Christ culture is the example that should be demonstrated through the God's ambassadors (i.e., the church). We do not have settle for lukewarm and ineffective cultural and/or racial sedatives to get by and become somewhat diverse.

---

[33] Bob Smietana, *Sunday morning in America is still segregated – and that's OK with worshippers*, found on http://lifewayresearch.com/2015/01/15/sunday-morning-in-america-still-segregated-and-thats-ok-with-worshipers/. Accessed on January 30, 2018.

We, as the church, can bring Christ culture to our communities, to our workplaces, to our schools, to our neighborhoods, and to each other.

It is at this point that we will now fix all of our attention on fleshing out and defining Christ culture in detail, so that we can effectively live out Christ culture in our daily lives, and collectively in and through our churches. While the rest of the world is arguing over which race is the most valuable, and which race owes which for what past indignity, we (the church) can be celebrating our life and freedom and salvation in Christ together, happily and joyfully sharing the beautiful aspects of our various human cultures with each other, and anxiously awaiting Christ's return and our eternities with Him.

As we look at Christ culture, we will examine what Christ culture is not, in the hopes that the contrast will make it all the clearer what Christ culture is, and we will investigate what Christ culture looks like in action as we journey through God's word and discover just who and what He wants the church to be in a lost and dark world that is divided by hatred and prejudice. Through Christ culture, the church can be the world changers that God wants us to be.

CHAPTER 6

CHRIST CULTURE
IS NOT RACIAL

For there is no difference between the Jew and the
Gentile: the same Lord is Lord of all and richly blesses
all who call on him.

—Romans 10:12 (NIV 1984)

Do not conform any longer to the pattern of this world,
but be transformed by the renewing of your mind. Then
you will be able to test and approve what God's will is –
his good, pleasing, and perfect will.

—Romans 12:2 (NIV 1984)

There is neither Jew nor Greek, slave nor free, male nor
female, for you are all one in Christ Jesus.

—Galatians 3:28 (NIV 1984)

If the local church is going to effectively bring Christ culture to its local
community, we must first and foremost allow God to renew our minds
when it comes to understanding different ethnicities and people groups.
As has been written time and again throughout this book, God did
not create, nor does biological science affirm, the allegation that there
is more than one race of people. Acts 17:26 goes further than that and
says that not only is there only one race of people, but God has made all
people of the same blood. Such a statement is not just a spiritual truth

for those who belong to Christ, but it is a matter of fact. If we all had complete genealogical records of our personal heritages and histories, we would all find ourselves ending up at Noah's ark, and going further, certainly back to the garden of Eden where human life began by the very hands of God. When we speak in terms of different races, we are, in words at least (however unintentional it may be), agreeing with Darwin and Sanger that not all people are indeed equal. And what's more, according to Darwin, Sanger, and American popular culture, certain people, depending on their race, are less human (less evolved) than others.

We speak in terms of different races of people because that is what we have been *taught by our culture*, but that is *not what we are taught by Christ* through His revealed word. What this hopefully disturbing reality teaches us about the state of the church in this area is that we have accepted the world's account of human relations over God's account. Author Ken Ham explains, "The Church tends to adopt man's ideas and then reinterprets scripture to fit those preconceived ideas. The result is that the Church is usually conformed to the world rather than transformed by the Word."[34] For much of American history, the church has seen people groups through the alternate reality of different races, and it is time that we stop seeing people as the world has presented them and start seeing people in the ways that God has intended.

A good start would be to realize that, since everyone is of one blood, when God brings people of a different culture or ethnicity across our paths, He is giving us an opportunity to welcome a member of our extended earthly family into God's heavenly family. How different might your church's community outreaches be if, instead of trying to reach a so-called different race, you were trying to reach members of your family who are lost? How might you approach them, and that kind of mission, differently? Overall, Christ culture will always transcend human culture in terms of unity among people because, in Christ, the relational chasms that separate people by human standards lose their divisive significance (Galatians 3:28).

A part of renewing our minds with respect to differences in ethnicity

---

[34] Ken Ham and A. Charles Ware, *One Race One Blood*, (Green Forest, AR: Master Books, 2013), 118.

and culture involves disconnecting a person's skin color from his or her culture. This is a critical element of Christ culture because skin color is often thought of interchangeably with a person's cultural background and personal behavior. And while there are various regions in America and throughout the world in which the people are predominantly one color, the color by itself is not an accurate indicator of culture, behavior, character, or sometimes even a person's ethnic heritage.

I (Andrew) have five children, and my wife and I make up an ethnically mixed marriage (I am black, and she is white), and so our kids are a beautiful combination of ethnicities from around the world. While four of our children are a brownish-tan type of skin tone, our youngest son is a blond-haired, blue-eyed, pale-skinned super-boy. Whenever I am out and about with my kids, it never fails that someone asks me how old my kids are, and who their little friend is. This line of questioning usually goes something like this:

> Checkout Person (noting all my kids): "Wow, you've really got your hands full there!"
>
> Me: "Yep." (What else can you say to that, really?)
>
> Checkout Person: "And who is their buddy, there?"
>
> Me: "That one belongs to me too."
>
> Checkout Person: "Really? ... Really? ... Really?" (expressing an increase of their mind being blown with each "really.")

It truly is an experience to watch people's faces as they try to reconcile how it would be possible for someone who looks like me to have a child who looks like my son. To be sure, I do not mind when people ask about my kids, or even when they do a double-take (so to speak) when they learn that they all are my kids, but it is a reminder that many people see other people in terms of, or in the bounds of (depending on the context), their skin color. I remember the first time I brought my five kids to my new church. I had just started on staff, and even some of the staff did not think that my little super-boy was indeed mine. Indeed a pale-skinned, blond-haired, and blue-eyed child does not immediately strike a person as being the offspring of a dark-skinned, dark-haired person, but it is true. And it doesn't just happen to my kids, as apparently, I am somewhat ethnically ambiguous as well.

My skin is a rich, brown tone, and I have big, physical build. I am asked often if I ever played football, or if I ever wrestled. My answer is yes, I played football high school until I broke my knee (which didn't take long since my knee broke on the second day of practice during my freshman year), and I do watch pro wrestling quite a bit, so there's that too. But I digress. Because of my physical appearance, I am perhaps equally asked (if not more so) if I am any of the following: Puerto Rican, Mexican, Cuban, or Samoan. I've had people come up to me and start speaking in Spanish because they assume I must be of some kind of Mexican heritage, and therefore the odds are good that I might speak (at least some) Spanish. Here again, people will tend to double-take when I share with them that I am not Mexican or Latin at all, and that I am mixed African American and European Caucasian. I've even had people argue with me about who my parents really were because they were thoroughly convinced of my heritage upon seeing me (those are amusing conversations too).

I share those examples with you to illustrate how easily—and without full awareness—we make assumptions about people based on the color of their skin and the culture that we associate with said skin tone. To be clear, our assumptions are not necessarily racist or even hostile. Nonetheless, we make assumptions about where people come from and the kind of people they are. Furthermore, churches do this as well when it comes to community and local outreach.

I have sat in many a church office and/or conference room and discussed with other pastors and church leaders how best to improve the particular church's outreach to their local community. What I remember the most about some of my earliest ministerial outreach efforts is not so much the effort itself, or even the result, but how much presumption went into our preparations. It is not uncommon for a church to be convicted about their lack of local community involvement. Lately, many church leaders are beginning to take seriously the importance of ministering cross-culturally within their own cities and towns, and so the ministry buzz-topic of being "ethnically diverse" and "multicultural" has become a growing outreach trend. One of the problems at this point in the outreach planning process is that, at least in my experience, when church leaders have talked about being "ethnically diverse" or "multicultural," what they really mean is that they want their churches to be more multicolored.

Granted, if the local is to reach its community with love of Christ, and its local community is a diverse split of ethnicities, skin tones, etc., it is reasonable to think that if we are reaching our community, our church population should look like what our community looks like. And with the aforementioned and clear self-segregation along color lines still present in the Christian church to this day, it is right that we should desire such diversity. But just like our skin can get a rash, which tells us that *something* is wrong, the condition of our skin does not tell us *what* is wrong. The same concept is true when it comes to the church. For the churches in ethnically diverse areas, if their congregations are not ethnically diverse, that is a symptom that something is wrong, but exactly what is wrong must be discovered prayerfully and carefully so that we do not fall to the temptation of thinking that just being a mix of skin colors, for the sake of skin color itself is going to make us effective again as a church.

And while we should not automatically fault the intentions of such a cause, we do need to examine the methods we use to execute said mission and determine whether we are being effective and/or even addressing the real issues.

What happens at times is that church leaders will gather to meet and discuss the problem and seek a solution. The solution is usually a big community event, or perhaps a short-term regular outreach accomplished by a team of volunteers and one or two church leaders. The problem I witnessed time and again was the fact that, while the church leaders would do some Internet research about the demographics of their communities, and even Google a few articles by big-name ministry leaders to get their insights, it was rare that the church would actually *go into* its community and *learn firsthand* about the people there. As such, the church has assumed that certain things are wrong within the community, and from those things they determine what they believe the needs of the community are, and they set out to meet those needs. But if the discovery of said needs comes, effectively, from Internet research, guilty emotions, and gut feelings, the result will likely be major church effort that yields very little, if any, fruit. And why is this? Because all too often, and for too many churches, we are putting all of our prayers and efforts into reaching the color of people's skin and not the condition of their souls.

Christ culture does not make personal distinctions based on the color of a person's skin, because in Christ culture, we understand that skin color is the least informative aspect of person's being. Granted, from people's skin we can sometimes tell if they've been working or playing outside; if symptoms are present, we can tell if a person might be ill or in pain; and we can tell if they are dealing with allergies, but that is about all. And of all the things that a people's skin color can tell us, it still tells us nothing about the character of people, nor does a cursory glance at anyone (or our communities) give us a clue about who God has designed them to be and/or what their needs might be at the moment.

Throughout this book, we have used terms like "racial reconciliation," and the like. We have used those terms, for the most part, because, as Americans, we will readily understand what is meant by them. In truth, since there is only one race of people, it may be more accurate to call this work, "cultural reconciliation," since we are trying to reconcile with people whose lifestyle cultures are different from our own. None of us were placed into a particular culture because we have a particular skin color. Rather, it is perfectly reasonable that any of us could have been any kind of skin color and still have been a part of the culture with which we are personally familiar.

Are we, as the church, willing to put down the goggles of racial division, through which we have been taught to see the world, and instead pick up the word of truth (i.e., the Bible) and see people as God intended? Part of what is so beautiful about the church is that the church is meant to be a picture of what eternity will be like with Christ. Is the current picture being portrayed by the American church accurate with respect to cultural reconciliation? Are we making disciples of all nations, or are we only making disciples of our personal favorite nations? Are our ethnic diversity outreach efforts skin deep, or soul deep? Your answers to those questions will make all the difference.

CHAPTER 7

CHRIST CULTURE ISN'T A PARTY

Freedom and justice cannot be parceled out in pieces to suit political convenience. I don't believe you can stand for freedom for one group of people and deny it to others.

—Coretta Scott King

The saddest part of the human race is we're obsessed with this idea of "us and them," which is really a no-win situation, whether it's racial, cultural, religious, or political.

—Dave Matthews

In American culture today, there is perhaps no force as divisive as politics. I would venture to suggest that politics even surpasses religion in that regard. Seemingly everywhere one may choose to look, people see the world through a political framework and/or ideology. For example, if I say the word *minority*, a person of color probably comes to your mind. But the term *minority* is a political identity assignment meant to keep politicians aware of the percentage of the "Black vote," the "Latino vote," and so on. And besides, other than percentage of population, what makes a person of color a minority? Even at this early juncture, we have segregated human beings on the basis of *skin color alone*, and we pronounce a verdict over their lives as to the types of opportunities they will have as they mature. Furthermore, we, as a people, make sweeping (usually overwhelmingly accusatory and negative) judgments about people, their character, their faith, their lifestyle, and much more on no other evidence than their political affiliation and/or political point of view. The challenge here is that political perspective has become so intertwined with Christian doctrine that many Christians measure the authenticity of a person's professed faith according to how they vote. And of course, such political discrimination pervades almost every aspect of life since, in our current American culture, virtually everything has been politicized and polarized to one degree or another.

As the political sphere in America has grown in its circumference, more and more people find larger and larger portions of their identities within the political ideas about which they are the most passionate, and Christians are not exempt from this observation. For Christians, perhaps the era that married Christianity with politics the most (within the last forty years) was the rise of the Moral Majority, a Christian political organization founded in 1979 by Dr. Jerry Falwell.[35] Responding to the massive cultural values shift that had taken place from the 1950s through the 1970s, Dr. Falwell organized American Christians in an effort to defend and uphold biblical social values through the ballot box. At that time in America, the church was still thought of an institution worthy of at least a modicum of respect and trust, and people would actively seek out a local church to find answers and healing for their lives. The Moral Majority was wildly successful in establishing Christians as a critically important voting voice, and in inspiring Christians to be more civically active.

Inasmuch as the Moral Majority helped to mobilize Christians during election seasons, it also has contributed to some unintended consequences concerning the marriage of politics and Christian doctrine that have made it difficult for the church to effectively minister cross-culturally in America.

---

[35] *Moral Majority,* found on Britannica.com/topic/Moral-Majority, accessed on April 5, 2018.

Unintended Consequence 1—Biblical Christians Turned into Political Evangelicals

When Jesus gave His disciples, and the church, their mission, He intended for Christians to be a sent people—that is, a people who actively engage with those who are lost (i.e., those who do not yet trust in Jesus for salvation). And for a large part of American history, the church was effective in reaching out to the lost and in need in society, and in living out their faith outside of a church building's walls. But as American culture began to grow bolder in a rejection of Christ, and as a gradual distrust in the church as an institution spread, the message of the church was increasingly drowned out in the midst of an ever-changing and increasingly political cultural climate. Those who were hostile toward the Christian church persisted in an accusatory smear campaign (that continues today) to label the church as antiquated and oppressive. It was in this climate that the Moral Majority entered the public scene.

The Moral Majority gave an increasingly ignored message a platform from which to be heard again. With the influence of biblical values now being a part of the national public discussion, Christians were once again emboldened to share the message of Christ confidently. Moreover, Christians were seeing their values reflected in the election stump speeches of civil leaders and politicians, a trend that helped jumpstart the birth and growth of the mega-church in America in the 1980s and '90s. While the rise of the Moral Majority led to a renaissance of socially conservative values, it also allowed space for Christians to come to expect their political leaders to legislate the biblical values they should have been actively living out.

As Christians pressed for a greater political presence in America, they did so at a sacrifice of a personal presence. More and more churches traded a ministry on Main Street for a voice on Pennsylvania Avenue, and in so doing, the public/political term *Evangelical* was born. To be sure, this term (in this context) was meant to identify a particular political affiliation, not a denominational one. An American Evangelical voter was now a part of a political voting demographic or voting bloc. Moreover, an American Evangelical (politically speaking) was someone who did not necessarily believe in the biblical tenants of Christianity but agreed with the general culturally relative morality that could, in some instances, be called "Christian." Ultimately, churches that were once vibrant and revolutionary forces in their cities, with rich histories of bringing all cultures together under the umbrella of Christ culture, began to settle for new histories of corporate achievement at the expense of action in their communities.

Through this time, the church had become comfortable relying on government to do what God asked the church to do. This is part of the reason why politics are such a divisive wedge in the first place, in that people, Christians included, seek too much from government, and when that government is threatened, it threatens them personally. And instead of chronicling a history and mission of tearing down the walls of division within their cities, many churches subtly shifted their focus to chronicling the history of how their own facility walls were built and expanded. All told, the more weight the church placed on politicians to be the public vessels of biblical values, the more the church became comfortable staying within their own walls (hence a reason for the desire to build them), only reaching out to those who ventured into their (the church's) pre-existing spheres of life.

Unintended Consequence 2—Christians Began to See the Lost Politically Instead of Personally

Perhaps the chief motivating factor in compelling one's compassion in to action on their behalf is how we see the other person. Or for example, in what kind of context do we interpret those around us? As Christians, our challenge is to see people the way that Christ sees them. However, because we are human beings who battle with our sinful flesh, we tend to take the world's word for it when it comes to the worth of people instead of God's. Interestingly enough, contrary to what the world may say, the world is actually a very religious place and people. This is not to say that all the world believes in the God of the Bible but that the world adheres to a pridefully religious attitude as it pertains to the treatment of others. For example, you have probably seen a movie or a television show depicting a group of people trying to gain access into a popular nightclub. They stand outside for hours, trying to get the bouncer's attention, and when they finally do, it turns out that, for whatever reason, they are not good enough to enjoy entry into the club. While such an example might be simplistic, it is also emblematic of how people treat each other, including Christians. And in modern American culture, there is possibly no more prevalent litmus test of acceptance than a person's political points of view.

As Christians became more and more politically active, they also began to see people through the political lenses with which they were interacting on an ever-increasing basis. Gradually, many Christians started seeing the lost according to their political affiliation as opposed to their tragic alienation from God. And with the wedge of politics dividing churches from their communities, the work of evangelism and bringing Christ's justice to the oppressed was diminished. Christians were both afraid of the new political cultural climate and afraid to engage with people whose politics were at odds with theirs.

Granted, some of these fears were well founded. It does not take a great deal of investigation to see that the American political culture is hostile toward biblical Christianity, and certainly to the name of Jesus. In truth, American culture today is doing all it can to rid itself of the God of the Bible, and to minimize the effects of His people (i.e., Christians). We live in a society that uses the political arm in an attempt to normalize sinful and destructive habits and addictions, while at the same time accusing the church through the same political arm of being bigoted and hateful. The church today is constantly facing threats of lawsuits and losing tax status, trying to defend herself against grossly inaccurate characterizations, and as mentioned previously, hard at work trying to earn back a trust from a society that loathes its very existence. So yes, Christians became afraid, and we approached people fearfully, if at all, and in some instances, we are at a loss as to how to effectively engage with our local communities.

Nonetheless, fear should not prevent the church from carrying out her God-given mission of reconciliation. Yet with the political atmosphere being more and more actively against Christianity, a damaging fear of each other is not a surprising result. So the Moral

Majority of the 1980s, in part, aimed to address this problem by taking the message from the church's pulpit to the community's platforms. However, instead of the community learning to see each other in a biblical way, the church learned how to see the lost in a political way, and it would appear that we remain stuck on this errant merry-go-round to this day.

As a pastor, I have the privilege helping people mature in their faith, and in equipping them to reach the lost around them. And yet, when speaking of the lost in society, I have time and again heard believers refer to the lost according to their (the lost's) politics far more than their personhood. This has created an altogether new evangelistic hurdle, which is to help Christians see the lost as a people without hope and in desperate need of Christ, and not as a people who are without sense and in desperate need of a political conversion. The world does not need more political pundits trying to win people to their agendas; the world needs more Christians on mission who proclaim and demonstrate the essential message of love and life in Christ alone.

In the four gospels of the New Testament, there is one story that is found in each one—that is, Jesus's feeding of the five thousand. Matthew 14, Mark 6, Luke 9, and John 6, all record this event. One of the most significant aspects of this miracle is the compassion that Jesus showed for people who were not at all like Him. When the story begins, Jesus is seeking rest to grieve because His beloved cousin, John the Baptist, had just been beheaded, and He had just received the horrible news. Be that as it may, a great crowd heard of Jesus's whereabouts and ultimately found Him. Now, the Bible records the count of the men in the crowds, which was five thousand. But it is likely that the crowd was between fifteen and twenty thousand people, including women and children, so this is not just a gathering of groupies. This is an entire sports arena of people who have tracked Jesus down.

Now, take a moment right here and put yourself in Jesus's place. Imagine that you have just been informed of the death of someone you love deeply, and you go to find some peace and quiet, but people follow you and ask you to help them. Most of us, understandably, would argue that there is too much on our minds and hearts to be able to offer any kind of help to anyone else. And of course, we are not Jesus, so there are some times when that may be true.

However, there are other times when we choose to keep our eyes focused on ourselves, and when we only have room for people who affirm us and not for those who need us to pour into them. Yet this is exactly what Jesus did. He poured into the crowds of people. Why? Because He saw them as God sees them (and of course, Jesus is God).

The book of Matthew says that Jesus had compassion on the people and healed their sicknesses. The book of Mark says that Jesus had compassion on the people and taught them for hours. The book of Luke says that Jesus proclaimed the gospel to the crowds and healed them, and the book of John says that Jesus saw that the people were hungry and made preparations to feed them. If we, as Christians, are going to learn how to see the lost as God does, and not how our political system does, then we should take a close look at this miracle because in it, Jesus modeled how His people are to see a lost and dying world.

Jesus Saw That the People Were Hurting—and He Did Something about It

The books of Matthew and Luke both record that Jesus healed the people of their illnesses and injuries. To be sure, let us not forget that Jesus Himself was in considerable emotional pain after the murder of John the Baptist, yet it was to the pain of the people that Jesus gave priority. Moreover, Jesus did not just acknowledge that the people were hurting. Rather, He took steps to lead them to healing. I (Andrew) do not know about you, but I have often heard Christians say the following phrase whenever they hear of someone in pain (can you already guess what it is?): "I'll pray for you." Certainly, prayer is powerful when offered to Christ in faith, but all too often, saying, "I'll pray for you" is just a Christianese way of saying, "Oh, that's too bad. I hope you get better, and don't bring this to me anymore." I mean sure, we feel a little bad that they are in pain, but we've got to finish grocery shopping and get the kids to bed so we can get back to work tomorrow, and so we end up offering only a momentary empathy without action. Jesus models just the opposite. Jesus did not dismiss the hurting people who were surrounding Him, even though He had an excuse that we would all understand and probably accept. Jesus's compassion for the people compelled Him to action because He saw them the way that God sees them.

Jesus Recognized the People's Thirst for Hope—and He Did Something about It

I (Andrew) would daresay that there is not a person in this world who would not agree that things are not as they should be in the world. We may not agree as to the reason why, but we all know that things are not right, and furthermore, that things need to be set right. The hope that is found in Jesus is that He will make right all that is wrong with a sin-infected creation. Jesus will soon make all things new, and one day, those who trust in Him will enjoy eternal life forever free from the presence and power of sin. Jesus paid for this hope by living a sinless life, dying on the cross, and raising to life again, never to return to the grave, and Jesus promises this hope for eternity to all those who will believe in Him. When faced with the crowds, Jesus saw a hopeless people, and He spent hours teaching them and proclaiming to them the hope of glory and the truth about the kingdom of God.

One of the reasons Jesus was so compelling as a teacher was that He demonstrated the very things He talked about. All through the towns that Jesus went through, stories of His healings and miracles preceded Him. Jesus did not merely rest on memorizing facts about God, and then trying to convince people about those facts. He lived them!

One of the detriments of such a political culture is the temptation to engage everyone in some kind of debate or argument. When we approach the message of the gospel in this way, we end up trusting our ability to recite to people memorized trivia about Christ as opposed to being able to demonstrate to others the triumphs of Christ in our lives. I (Andrew) am convinced that people today do not care about how much we know about Christ, but rather, they want to know how Christ has transformed our lives, and how He has given us a hope that we hold onto even in the midst of a culture that no longer wants us around. What people need to see from Christians is how the word of God has shaped their lives, and how the compassion of Christ has changed how they see the people of this world. No one really cares if we can win on Bible Jeopardy. The temptation to learn facts to win an argument has stunted the church's ability to effectively proclaim salvation in Christ and the kingdom of God. To be sure, we do need to be literate in terms of scripture, but we also need to be active in terms of our own discipleship so when we are faced with the crowds, we can address their need for hope with the message of gospel and not a mere recitation of trivia.

Jesus Saw That the People Were Physically Hungry—and He Did Something about It

John 6 describes the aftermath of the feeding of the five thousand. John records that Jesus invited the crowds to believe in Him but that the crowds rejected Him and went away disappointed. Wait a minute ... what? Jesus healed them, He taught them, He fed them miraculously, and they still rejected Him? And what's more, He let them go?

One of the things that keeps Christians from investing in others is the fact that we do not know what kind of return our investment will bring. Christians love stories of outreach events that brought about multiple "decisions for Christ." Yet the outreach events where no one "came to faith" are usually seen as failures that need re-tooling. Jesus held a picnic in the park and there were twenty thousand people in attendance, and when it was all said and done, only twelve people remained with Jesus, and those twelve were the same twelve who were with Jesus to begin with. According to modern church logic, Jesus should go back to the drawing board and try again next summer. Yet although the masses were not moved to receive Christ as Lord, this was not a failure. The real failure would have been if Jesus had seen the needs of the people and had done nothing at all.

When Jesus addressed the crowds, He did not see Republicans and Democrats, or conservatives and liberals. He did not see Code Pink and the NRA, or unions, or Hispanics, or Asians, or Blacks, or Jews.

Jesus saw people. Jesus saw His creation, who were lost because of sin, and who were in danger of entering eternity under God's wrath and not His mercy. Jesus saw His lost children were hurting, and so He healed them humbly. Jesus saw that His lost children were without hope, and so He taught them truthfully. And Jesus saw that His lost children were physically hungry, and so He fed them abundantly. And the people Jesus served that day did not know Him outside of His reputation. The people Jesus served that day did not agree with His points of view. Yet Jesus touched them, talked with them, and ate with them. Contrast that to the church today, wherein Christian Republicans have a hard time sitting in the same pews with Christian Democrats, let alone talking with each other, or sharing a meal together.

Here's a thought: How many church outreaches do you think have not even gotten off the ground because the Christians who are putting on the outreach are afraid of not getting a "spiritual return"? Or how about this: How many churches do you think line the streets of towns and communities whose effective outreach does not get past their own property lines? I (Andrew) submit that as long as we continue to see people according to a worldly evaluation structure, we will continue to struggle to effectively and faithfully meet the needs of the lost in our cities, and/or to break down the self-imposed cultural barriers that are keeping us apart. But if we will follow the example of Christ and recognize that everyone who is lost is hurting, hungry, and without hope, we may be better able to reach them with the love of Christ that they so desperately need, and that only the church can bring.

Questions to consider: When we, as Christians, see the lost in need in our communities, what are we doing about it? When we see the lost in our communities trapped behind the oppressive walls of cultural division, what are we doing about it? The answers to these questions will differ from community to community in America, but we pray that our love for Christ will compel us into action so that we, as the church, will have an answer at all.

Unintended Consequence 3—Political Affiliation Has Become a New Racial Classification

One of the practical reasons that discrimination and prejudice are so difficult to fight is that discrimination is entirely subjective from person to person. As we have already discussed in previous chapters, prejudices concerning any matter (skin color, status, nationality, etc.) come from the sinful hearts of prideful human beings, and every human being has their own standard of right and wrong and acceptable and unacceptable. So when we approach the matter of prejudices and preferences regarding political points of view, it stands to reason that there would be varying degrees of discrimination, from the obnoxiously overt to the subliminally subtle. With that much being said, our culture today, and many Christians, make the same kinds of character and worth judgments about people based on their politics as has been known to occur concerning one's skin color.

For example, a recent story surfaced in virtually every major (and minor) news outlet chronicling a woman in Sacramento, California, who refuses to sell her home to anyone who supports the current president.[36], [37] The woman in question cites her belief that anyone (again, anyone) who supports the current president must be of such low moral quality that she is not able to live with the thought of someone who voted differently than she did living in her home after she is long gone. I wonder how many who might one day read this book can imagine hating one aspect of a person so much that they are unwilling to have anything at all to do with anyone else who may also share such an attribute. Moreover, does not this kind of hate sound an awful lot like the kind of hatred that might have inspired the bombing of the Williams' house in Memphis, Tennessee, in 1953? What is the difference between, "I don't want any black people moving into my neighborhood!" and "I don't want any Republicans buying my house

---

[36] Megan Cerullo, *California Woman Refuses to Sell Home to a Trump Supporter*, found on http://www.nydailynews.com/news/national/california-woman-refuses-sell-home-trump-supporter-article-1.3907232. Accessed on 4/12/2018

[37] At the time of this writing, Donald Trump is the current president of the United States.

and moving into my neighborhood"? Prejudice is prejudice no matter the preference upon which it may be based.

In our experience, we have found that the American church has an equally difficult time getting past a person's politics as well, and this is true of all political ideologies that are represented in the church. Granted, there are far too many churches that allow their political ideological morality to dictate their theology, doctrine, and practice, but at the same time, there are genuinely theologically sound churches that see the world through different political persuasions. We have observed a few small group discussions in my time in ministry start off united in the Bible and end up divided over politics. Curiously, when that happens in the context of the church, it seems like Christians are more concerned with convincing people to vote "correctly" than they are with helping people live righteously as they follow Christ. As a result, in addition to the color lines that exist in the church, there are distinct political lines that exist as well. And adding political divides to the cultural divides within the church only weakens our already limited ability to reach across cultural lines.

Ask yourself these questions: Would you join a church that was politically (not doctrinally) different from you? How many of your friends differ politically from you? Are you able to have political conversations without the conversation dissolving into an insult-filled argument (include your Facebook and Twitter accounts too)? Would you be willing to see someone on the other side of the political aisle not as a threat, but as someone who Jesus loved so desperately that He died for them just like He died for you?

What Can We Make of All This So Far?

In surveying the evidence presented in this book so far, it is our prayer that you (the reader) can see these five things clearly:

1. All of the "ism" discrimination problems that we face are symptoms of our sin.

2. The more that humanity has tried to engineer the perfect culture through laws and social experimentation, the more the culture has fragmented, split, and segregated.
3. The racial, class, and political wars are all aspects of the larger culture wars between people.
4. God's battle plan to transcend the earthly culture wars was won in the work of Christ's death and resurrection and is carried out through those who believe in Him (i.e. the church).
5. The church's mission on earth is to introduce people to Jesus, and to adopt them into Christ culture.

It is at this point in our journey that we turn fully to the picture of what Christ culture truly is. We will leave the ugliness of human depravity behind and focus on the glory of God and how He loves and empowers believers to be able to live in Christ culture, even among the human culture wars that plague our cities and communities. We will journey through different parts of scripture to see the life that God intended us to live on earth as we await the glorious eternity to come. And together in our local churches, we will learn how we can practically begin to address the cultural divisions in our own cities so that the church might be as Jesus said:

You are the light of the world. A town built on a hill cannot be hidden. Neither do people light a lamp and put it under a bowl. Instead they put it on its stand, and it gives light to everyone in the house. In the same way, let your light shine before others, that they may see your good deeds and glorify your Father in heaven. (Matthew 5:14–16 NIV 2011)

CHAPTER 8

CHRIST CULTURE IS LOVING THOSE WHO YOU THOUGHT WERE BENEATH YOU

> I have a dream that one day on the red hills of Georgia, the sons of former slaves and the sons of former slave owners will be able to sit together at the table of brotherhood.
>
> —Dr. Martin Luther King Jr.

If we, as the church, are going to effectively break down the culture barriers, whether they are found in our communities, our churches, or personally, we need to recognize that we will be ambassadors of reconciliation for people whom we otherwise might prefer to ignore, if not leave out altogether. On the surface, we may not say that we think anyone is necessarily "beneath" us, yet if we are honest with ourselves about ourselves, we will identify a person, or maybe a type of person, with whom we wish we did not have to engage, and those are the people who we feel, no matter how aware we may be, are beneath us. Christians, for some of us, these people may be in our cities, for others they may be in your own church body, and for others, they may be in your own family.

The quote that led this chapter is profound—not because it was said by Dr. King, or because it was said during a time of civil upheaval, but because it calls for a day when people of seemingly opposite cultures might see and treat each other as equals. Here again, it must be restated that our problems with racism and so on are really culture problems. And the truth remains that until we are willing to submit to Christ and set aside those parts of our personal and social cultures that only serve to prohibit others, prejudice and discrimination will remain not just in American life, but in the life of the church.

One of the smallest books in the entire Bible is the book of Philemon. Philemon was a letter written by the apostle Paul to a Christian slave owner (Philemon) who lived in Asia Minor. Paul wrote Philemon and urged him to welcome back his runaway slave, Onesimus, who had recently become a Christian after a meeting with Paul while Paul was in prison. Philemon is perhaps one of the most important when seeking to understand just what Christ culture is and what Christ culture requires of believers to live in it faithfully.

Because of the woeful topic and practice of slavery throughout world history, the real power of Paul's letter can get lost in the immediate sensational surface tension of slaves and slave owners. Certainly, many of those critical of the Bible, and even some Christians, have pushed back at the Bible's addressing of the issue of slavery because the Bible appears to have a distinct lack of abolitionist language in its text. And it is true that Paul did not ask Philemon to set his slave free, which, on the surface, might appear to be more harsh than heavenly. After all, if Onesimus had run away and was no longer with his slave owner, why is it merciful of Paul to request for Onesimus to *return* to his slave master? What Paul understood is what Christians need to grasp in order to be obedient ambassadors of Christ culture: to free the oppressed, Christ must transform the heart of the oppressor. And it was to this end that Paul made his appeal.

As has been alluded to, Onesimus was a slave who ran away from his slave owner and who also apparently stole from his slave owner just before he made his escape. The apostle Paul was in prison during this time, and at some point, his path crossed with that of Onesimus. Paul would proclaim the gospel to Onesimus, and Onesimus would receive salvation in Christ Jesus, as is written when Paul calls Onesimus his "son" (Philemon v. 10). At this time and place in world history, there was no more reviled part of humanity than a runaway slave. Runaway slaves would often have difficulty finding long-term refuge as very few would even consider housing them for one hour, let alone an indefinite period of time. And of course, being a runaway slave meant that one could not get work, buy a house, rent a hotel, etc. While not much can be known for certain as to the exact specifics surrounding Paul and Onesimus's introduction, somehow Onesimus met Paul while Paul was in prison. Was Onesimus a prisoner? Did Onesimus run to hide out in a prison? There is no clear evidence either way, but it is clear that the freedom that Onesimus sought had not come to fruition thus far, especially if he found himself in/at a prison.

While Christians today might not be able to relate to the slave/slave master contrast, we can certainly relate to the marriage of cultures that the apostle Paul was petitioning for. Consider the fact that Paul, the author of the letter, was a Jew, at one time the highest of the Pharisees, next to whom there was no religious equal. Philemon was a Gentile who came from wealth and privilege, and of course Onesimus was a runaway slave.[38] Make no mistake, at the time of the writing of Philemon, it was still quite a significant event that a Jew, a Gentile, and a runaway slave would be in the same social circles, let alone the same literary sentence. Christians today may not be able to relate to slave/slave master, but we can certainly relate to seemingly unmixable cultures converging under the umbrella of the church.

Now, here's where the story gets good. The apostle Paul began his petition for Onesimus by calling Onesimus "his very heart" (v. 12), indicating a deep love for Onesimus, which again, must be acknowledged in the light of their very different cultures. A Jew of the highest order does not love, let alone spiritually adopt, a runaway slave, but Paul did. Paul was also careful not to have Philemon respond to his request out of obligation or duty. At the time of the writing, Paul certainly could have "pulled rank" as an important founder of the early Christian church, but instead, Paul appealed to Philemon out of Christian love.[39] Christian scholar Arthur A. Rupprecht writes, "(Philemon) is to be motivated by (Christian love) … (and that out of that)… should come more than mere

---

[38] Rupprecht, A. A. (1981). Philemon. In F. E. Gaebelein (Ed.), *The Expositor's Bible Commentary: Ephesians through Philemon* (Vol. 11). Grand Rapids, MI: Zondervan Publishing House.

[39] Ibid.

reconciliation."[40] In verse 21, Paul writes that he is sure that Philemon will do much more than he is asking him (Philemon) to do. Implying that not only will Philemon reconcile kindly with Onesimus, but he will give him freedom because of the love of Christ that binds them in unity. And there it is.

The bonds of slavery and oppression are broken, not by the laws of the land, but by the love of Christ in the hearts of people, transforming and compelling them to Christlike action, and moving them into Christ culture together.

One of the objections to the idea that prejudice must be dealt with at the heart/spiritual level is because many people do not understand that love is more than a feeling or an emotion; love is actually a powerful, compelling, and undeniable force that leads those who submit to it to freedom and life in Christ, because as it is written, "God is love" (1 John 4:8). At the same time, too many Christians mistake intellectual agreement with God for actually loving Him and applying His truths in their lives. This is how the church can remain the most segregated institution in American society long after the demise of national slavery, segregation, and Jim Crow laws. The church has agreed that slavery and discrimination are wrong, but overall, we have not applied that truth to our lives as a universal body of believers, and therefore we remain separated into our own cultures, having not yet tasted the freedom that Paul writes about in his letter to Philemon. Jesus Christ is quite clear that if we love Him, we will obey Him. In other words, if our love for Christ is real, it will compel us to action according to His truth, mercy, and justice.

As a universal church in America, has our love for Christ grown stale? Well, in terms of breaking down culture walls and overcoming the oppression therein, it would appear so. I (Andrew) am not sure about you, but when I first began studying the book of Philemon, I studied from Paul's perspective, and I put myself in Paul's place. I was the wise Christian who wanted to contend for the oppressed, and who wanted to positively affect for Christ's sake the shackles of injustice that hold so many people hostage to this day.

While it is right and good for Christians to take on the heart of

---

[40] Ibid.

Paul, I have come to learn that my closest place in this story is with Philemon. And what changed for me was when I investigated what Philemon learned from this circumstance as opposed to focusing only on what the apostle Paul (or for that matter, I) already knew. So let's do that together. If you have a Bible handy, take a read through the book of Philemon (it's super short) and then come back to this spot in the book. As you read, think of yourself as Philemon and God as Paul, and think of a person or type of people that you would prefer to ignore in your life as Onesimus.

Welcome back. Okay, let's take a look at what Philemon learned and connect that what it means to live in Christ culture.

Philemon Acknowledged Paul's Apostolic Authority (v. 8)

While Paul did not "order" or otherwise force Philemon to respond favorably to his request, Paul's authority in the church was not unnoticed or misunderstood by Philemon. This is critical because, in his apostolic authority, Paul is giving a "new dignity to the slave class,"[41] something that would have been a revelation to Philemon at the time. What we need to understand is that God has all authority, and it is God who gives dignity and worth to people. The question to us is whether we will acknowledge such authority and respond accordingly, or if we choose to continue to ignore God's absolute right to ask us to receive the "runaway slaves" of our communities. Just like Paul did not force Philemon's response, God does not force our response either, wanting us to obey out of our love for Him instead of compulsion. Think about that for a second. The very person you would rather not deal with just may the very person that God is asking you to receive in His name.

---

[41] Ibid.

Philemon Learned That Onesimus Is a Child of God, Just Like He Is (v. 10–16)

Because of the unity of humanity that is only possible through Christ, Paul is able to ask Philemon to begin to see Onesimus not as a slave, but as a brother in the Lord, which flows out of their common faith in Christ. Furthermore, Paul asks Philemon to see Onesimus as a fellow man, implying not only their equality in Christ but also their equality in humanity as creations of God. Last, Paul pleads with Philemon to see Onesimus as a partner, a word that, in the Greek, has the sense of "business partner" or "partner in ministry."[42] In other words, Paul is asking Philemon to receive Onesimus as he might "receive Paul himself."[43] When one meditates on and truly contemplates those words from the apostle Paul, one cannot help but hear the echoes of Jesus Christ Himself saying that "what we do to the least of His people, we do to Him" (Matt. 25:40). When we faithfully, humbly, and obediently receive those in our cities whom God is asking us to adopt, we are, in this sense, welcoming Christ Himself.

Who is your Onesimus right now? A coworker? Perhaps a group of people in your city that God has been reminding you about in your spirit lately? A family member? Do you have any fear of their culture overwhelming your current, existing culture? For example, if you really reach out to person X, do you have any concern that they may not fit in with you and/or your friends at church? If so, you may want to ask yourself this question: Does Jesus want person X to fit in, or does He want you to make room for them to be adopted into His family, and into your church family specifically?

It is unspeakably sobering to realize that before God we are no different than the people and/or cultures we are either uncomfortable with, or that we might even despise. And yet God's vision for people has always been that multiple cultures would come together as one people, and that all those cultures would come under the lordship of one culture, Christ culture. In Christ culture, we leave behind the divisive parts of our cultures and share the beautiful parts of our cultures

---

[42] Ibid.

[43] Ibid.

together. Inasmuch as the thought of leaving behind certain parts of our cultures may give us pause, one must also wonder if the sharing of other cultures frightens us as well. What if my new friends do not appreciate or enjoy the things that I enjoy? What if I don't identify with their interests? And so on. It may be helpful, convicting, or challenging to know that the question really is not about our ability to culturally fit in with others, or to make others culturally fit in with us, but whether we are willing to submit our personal cultures to Christ's culture.

Philemon Learned Humility by Accepting Repayment from Paul Instead of Onesimus (v. 18–19)

While it is reasonably accepted that Onesimus likely stole something or some things from Philemon, it is possible that Onesimus owed Philemon some other kind of debt (perhaps Philemon lost wages from the lost work that Onesimus would have done had he not run away). At any rate, Onesimus is in debt to Philemon, and this debt must be settled. Here again, Paul intercedes and tells Philemon that he will pay whatever Onesimus owes. Moreover, Paul reminds Philemon that he is indebted to him as it is anyway. In this way, Paul does for Onesimus and Philemon what Christ has done for everyone who believes in Him; he paid their debt.

As it pertains to building cultural bridges and cultural reconciliation, one of the greatest challenges is getting past the past hurts and wrongs that we have done to each in generations past and present. Certainly, those Americans who grew up through slavery and segregation will pass on a different legacy point of view to their children and grandchildren than will those Americans who did not experience the same. Sometimes the injustices of generations past can still echo pains and hurts for years into the future. How do we deal with this seemingly insurmountable problem? In the present, we wade through harmful stigmas that were first put in place in the past. Those who wronged others in the past may not be alive to ask for forgiveness and seek relational repair. On the other hand, what if our hurt and pain are actually *keeping* us from wanting reconciliation in the first place?

When Paul proposed to Philemon the notion of him paying Onesimus's debt, he was asking Philemon not hold that debt against him. It is difficult for human beings to accept justice when it does not come in the form that we, as individuals, might prefer or believe to be best. Forgiveness seems to let the perpetrator off the hook, so to speak, and potentially dismisses all hope of full justice ever being brought to bear. So to allow someone else to pay a price on behalf of another is not a small thing to do for anyone.

When Jesus died on the cross, He paid a debt to God for our sin. Granted, it was a debt that we could not pay, and it was a debt for which we were guilty, not Jesus. Yet God accepted the sacrifice of Jesus on the cross to restore relationship with created humanity.

In terms of human forgiveness, God works in a similar way, and when we extend that work to cultural reconciliation through the church, we need to be prepared to submit to the justice that God wants to bring to us through Christ.

God has most definitely presented you with an opportunity to cross the cultural lines in your community at one time or another. And likely, crossing one of those cultural lines meant dealing with a fear, or a past hurt, that you now associate with that painful or threatening culture. If God brought someone from said culture to you and asked you to receive them, and if He told you that He will take care of the debt of pain that is owed to you, would that be enough for you? Would you acknowledge God's authority to do so? Would you see the other person as loved by God just like you? Would you see God's justice as sufficient in paying for whatever debt of apology (or otherwise) that you feel is owed to you?

Imagine Dr. King's dream of the children of slaves and the children of slave owners sharing a table of brotherhood together. Imagine what is required of everyone involved for that dream to come true. The children of slaves would have to forgive the children of the slave owners. The children of the slave owners would have to see the children of the slaves as absolute equals in every way, and even as their own family. Both sides would have to come to *the same table*, *at the same time*, and *partake together* in fellowship. And since there is no way that the children of the slave owners could ever repay the children of the slaves for the injustices of the past, all involved would have to accept the payment and justice that is offered in and through Jesus Christ. Dr. King's dream was one that he would not readily see in his lifetime, yet centuries before, halfway around the world, the apostle Paul asked Philemon and Onesimus to embody that very dream. And the only way that would be possible was, and still is, through Christ. After all, we are talking about Christ culture.

CHAPTER 9

CHRIST CULTURE IS LUNCH TOGETHER

All great change in America begins at the dinner table.
—Ronald Reagan

One of the great turning points in one's life is deciding at which table one should eat lunch in high school. Stereotypically speaking, there are the jocks, the cheerleaders, the band geeks, the mathletes, the glee club, the weird kids that collect bugs, the student council kids, the outcasts, the troublemakers, and you. It goes without saying that the choice you make at this juncture can determine greatly how your last years as an adolescent will go.

As for me (Andrew), if I wasn't sitting by myself, I usually sat with a crew of students who got into misdemeanor-style trouble. That is, they were not the rough kids at school, but they did cut class, pull pranks, and appear with some regularity in detention. Originally, I wanted to sit with the jocks, but when you break your knee at the second day of football practice, your stock as a respected athlete becomes somewhat diminished. I had musical talent, and I could sing, which was good at school assemblies but less effective in achieving the "cool" status that I coveted. And so it was that I found some friends who liked me well enough to include me in their hangouts and toilet paper adventures (we TP'd a fair amount of houses in our day), and it was with this group that I would eat lunch now and then.

It is a most peculiar and interesting thing how much it matters with whom we regularly share meals. When we eat with people it demonstrates publicly who we care about, the things we affirm, and what/who is important to us. When seen in that light, eating is actually a very intimate, yet outward expression of our inward motivations, feelings, priorities, and values. Without a doubt, my classmates in school drew certain conclusions about me based on with whom I shared a lunch table at school.

The compelling factor in "choosing a lunch table," whether figuratively or literally, is precisely how much weight and importance we place on the opinions of those who are *not at our lunch table*. Indeed, when choosing a lunch table back in high school, I wanted to sit at the table that I thought would look the best to *others*, not necessarily to those with whom I was sitting, or even to myself. My motivation was to look as "cool" as I could to as many people who did not know me as possible.

In our lives, there are those people whose opinions of us matter the most. And as people who want their approval, we base some of the values of our lives, whether for a season (like high school) or for longer, on those outside opinions. Granted, sometimes outside opinions are important, like those that keep us accountable in a biblical manner, but apart from that, usually those outside opinions have the effect of trapping us in our own fears and insecurities. As a result, we end up slaves to our fears, allowing the ever-changing views of others to dictate the steps we take in our lives as opposed to the freeing love of Christ.

In our experience, we have found that while everyone fights these battles of influence to one degree or another, one group of people that are especially vulnerable are leaders, and of that group, church leaders. Political leaders may be vulnerable to corruption and underhanded influence, but church leaders (i.e. pastors, lay leaders, ministry directors, etc.) are vulnerable to the constant opinions and pressure that is placed upon them from the very people they have dedicated their lives to serve. The apostle Peter is a prime example of that about which we are speaking. Peter, throughout his early ministry, was plagued with a fear of man—that is, a fear of what people thought of him. Ultimately, Peter's fear was so crippling that he denied knowing Christ three times on the very day of Jesus's crucifixion.

While Peter's denial of Christ was certainly a high-water mark of his struggle with fear of man, it would not be the last time he would fight that battle. Even as Peter would speak boldly at Pentecost, and be constantly imprisoned for his faith in Jesus, Peter was still hesitant to minister to Gentiles. Peter was a Jew, and as a Jew, while Peter did not have an overly discriminatory training in his faith, he had his own inherited cultural prejudices against the Gentiles with which to contend. Of course, since Peter had been following Christ, his own prejudices were beginning to soften, yet he remained timid with respect to ministering to anyone other than his own Jewish people.

In Acts 10, Peter was on his way to Cornelius's (a Roman Gentile believer) house upon Cornelius's request. The biblical account details how, as Peter was praying, he became hungry and soon fell into a trance (v. 10). In his trance, Peter saw a vision of four-footed animals of all kinds, both those that would be considered clean by Jewish traditional standards (those that chewed the cud and had cloven hoofs) and those that would have been considered unclean, comingled together along with reptiles and birds.[44] What shocked Peter about this dream is that, in the dream, Peter heard a message from God telling him (Peter) to "kill and eat" (v. 13). The point of contention that Peter had with this command was that it did not specify which animals he should kill and eat, and as a Jew, he was not to eat any animal that was considered unclean. Yet now, Peter was being told by God that it was okay to eat what he formally thought was unclean. What an earth-shattering revelation! Furthermore, God told Peter not to call anything unclean that He had made clean. To be sure, the specific application of this vision had to do with Jewish dietary regulations, but in the not-too-distant future, Peter would learn the fullest extent and ramifications of this revelation (i.e., the future mixing of Jews and Gentiles in the new Christian church).

Once he arrived at Cornelius's house, Peter and Cornelius began a monumental exchange of dialogue chronicling the renewing of their minds that was taking place at that moment. Peter brought up the fact that it was against the law for a Jew like Peter to spend time with or

---

[44] Longenecker, R. N. (1981). The Acts of the Apostles. In F. E. Gaebelein (Ed.), *The Expositor's Bible Commentary: John and Acts* (Vol. 9). Grand Rapids, MI: Zondervan Publishing House.

visit a Gentile like Cornelius. However, Peter, recognizing that it was God who was orchestrating this coming together of segregated cultures, submitted to God's will and command and practiced (as well as taught) the biblical fact that God does not show favoritism to any particular people.

In Acts 11, Peter explained his actions to the believers in Jerusalem who had heard of what Peter had done. Peter articulated the truth that all people are equal before God, and that all people have equal access to His salvation. As the biblical narrative continues, we read about the church's expansion including both Jews and Gentiles, and the evangelistic efforts of Peter, Paul, and Barnabas. Paul and Barnabas would soon be brought before the Jewish leaders at the Council of Jerusalem (Acts 15) for preaching salvation to the Gentiles, at which Peter defended Paul and Barnabas, and the council would send a letter welcoming Gentiles into the faith.

Fast forward a little bit to Galatians 2, and we are invited into a scene wherein Peter is now regularly eating with the Gentiles. In fact, Peter the Jew lived most of his life like a Gentile, and not like the religiously pious Jews of his heritage. No sooner was this taking place than some high-ranking Jews join the believers at the scene. At the appearance of these Jews, Peter began to distance himself from the Gentiles, more and more refusing to eat with them, or even acknowledge them. Moreover, Peter's actions influenced other believers, including Barnabus, who, following Peter's lead, began to retreat from the Gentiles into a decidedly Jewish camp of friends (v. 13). And just like in high school cafeterias across America, Peter is choosing his lunch table according to what others think of him. Peter's motivation is dominated by his own fear and insecurity, and in this display, he is publicly admitting that he would rather look good in front of a few religious people than to obey the command that God had given him in the vision at Cornelius's house.

Just imagine this scene for a second and put yourself in the place of one of the Gentiles who had been eating with Peter. You would have heard of how Peter has stood up and defended Gentile inclusion and how Peter himself had changed with respect to his views of Gentiles and Gentile believers. Not only that, but you would now be hanging out with the guy who walked with Jesus for three years, who walked on water, who was among the first to see the empty tomb after the resurrection of Christ, and who had been miraculously set free from prison several times. This guy (Peter) is a rock star in the early church (quite literally; Jesus nicknamed Peter, "rock" in Matthew 16:13–20), and now Peter is hanging out with you, a Gentile.

All of a sudden, some Jews start hanging around the cafeteria, and Peter starts avoiding and ignoring you. You can likely tell that Peter wants to impress his Jewish friends, but you thought Peter was your friend too. And why did he Peter feel the need to impress his Jewish friends at your expense? Would you not feel confused, hurt, and even a little betrayed?

Regrettably, I (Andrew) have seen such fear of man displayed in church leaders and pastor that I have worked with and/or met with at various points over my time in local ministry. I have been turned down for a position at a few different churches because my skin is brown, and certain people would be uncomfortable at a church with a pastor whose skin is darker than theirs. Now, it is one thing for a few people in a church congregation to think that way, and it is still another for the leaders to be so concerned with such prejudice that it dictates how they proceed with ministry. For leaders of any kind to acquiesce to requests that are so obviously born out of sin reflects a failure of leadership, and, like Peter, a crippling fear of man. Do we really follow the Lord when, to avoid uncomfortable conflict, we avoid confronting prejudice and sinful pride in those we serve and love?

To be sure, prejudices like these are not always rooted in hate, but fear, albeit, that does not excuse the sin. The people in question in my experience did not hate me or even want me to leave per se, but they had a deep and ingrained unease with worshiping that closely with someone from a different cultural background. The same is true with Peter in the instances described above. It is not as though Peter hated Gentiles. In fact, just the opposite was true, but when faced with the pridefully religious rigidity of certain traditional Jews among them, Peter wilted under the pressure and failed. And Peter's failure was not without consequence, as he led many other Jewish believers astray as a result of his fear.

Now, it just so happened that the apostle Paul was also among the believers gathered at Antioch, and Paul, seeing Peter's folly, rebuked him accordingly. Before examining Paul's rebuke of Peter, it is important to note that Paul did not enjoy arguing, and certainly was not looking to publicly besmirch the apostle Peter, rather, Paul's concern was for the truth of the gospel, and in Peter's fear, Peter compromised the proclamation of God's truth.[45] With the aforementioned as Paul's motivation, we can learn, just like Peter did, what it means to actively and obediently apply the principles of Christ culture.

Principle 1—Teaching the Whole Gospel Demands that Christians Apply It as Well as Agree with It

In Galatians 2:14, Paul says that he witnessed Peter not living according to the truth of the gospel. In other words, Peter's actions were teaching a false gospel that certain Christian groups are superior, or more holy, than other ones. There is no doubt that Peter believed in salvation through Christ alone, but by choosing one group to the exclusion of another, he undercut his own conviction and thus brought disunity into the new church.

It is not a secret that Jesus wants His followers to make disciples of all nations, but how can we do that if we only reach out to those whose cultures are the same as ours? Moreover, how can we do that effectively if we favor one kind of culture over another? I know of a great many churches that house other, smaller churches on their property, and usually these other churches are of a different cultural and/or ethnic background than the host church. Now, having been a pastor and having planted a church, I am all for churches lending a helping hand to the passing church that needs a place to land and grow from time to time. But what about those churches that are looking for a permanent place to meet? Could it be that God is giving the host church an opportunity to assimilate those believers into their larger body of believers, and in

---

[45] Boice, J. M. (1976). Galatians. In F. E. Gaebelein (Ed.), *The Expositor's Bible Commentary: Romans through Galatians* (Vol. 10). Grand Rapids, MI: Zondervan Publishing House.

so doing, for the larger church to assimilate into the new culture of the guest church?

I believe that the American church has left far too many opportunities to demonstrate Christ culture in this way sitting on the table (so to speak), untouched and untried, and this is to the detriment of our broader culture. Just imagine what kind of testimony it would send to the watching world if the American church learned how to truly unite different cultures under the banner of Christ culture. Think of the impact we could have in our communities if, for example, when the small Spanish language Baptist church wanted to rent space from the larger First Baptist Church, the First Baptist Church set out to learn how to speak Spanish to fully adopt the Spanish church as a direct part of their church family. And it stands to reason that the members of the Spanish church might be inclined to strengthen their English-speaking skills should they be welcomed with such intentional love and respect.

We, that is, Christians, so often forget the magnitude of what it meant that God came to earth in the Person of Jesus Christ and how that magnitude of meaning should influence our ministry today. First, Jesus left His world and came to ours. How often do we leave our own worlds and reach out to a different one? Second, Jesus spoke our language and respected our human cultures. How often do we learn the language and culture of the community next to us within our own city? Third, Jesus modeled surrender to us. How often do we sacrifice our sacred cows for the sake of the lost in our neighborhoods? It is easy to say, "Amen, Pastor!" when we hear a powerful truth on Sunday, but it is quite another thing to apply that truth in our lives precisely because of the sacrifice that it will require of us. Nonetheless, this principle is non-negotiable if we are to faithfully live in Christ culture together as one people.

Principle 2—Hypocrisy Is Born Out of Fear; Unity Is Born Out of Faith

In verses 14–16 of Galatians 2, Paul calls out Peter's hypocrisy in excluding the Gentiles from fellowship. Not only was Peter showing favoritism, but he was pretending to live a life that he did not live, demanding that the Gentiles live like the Jews even though he did not do so himself. Peter's fear of man resulted in placing obstacles in front of people who would otherwise enjoy fellowship with everyone in the freedom and liberty that was won in Christ on the cross. And the more obstacles and barriers that we build out of fear, the more divided we ultimately become.

Have you ever wondered why some Christians who believe so strongly about a certain thing, demand it of others far more strictly than they do of themselves? Or how Christians can fiercely disdain one kind of worship practice or another, yet, instead of rebuking said practice, they just make sure that they never have to participate in it? Do you think that maybe the divisions that we have among ourselves over matters such as these actually arise from our own fears and insecurities? With that said, if it really is such heresy to sing a Chris Tomlin (for example) song as some Christians have contended, should not their hearts break for those Christians who sing from Mr. Tomlin's catalog? Interestingly, instead of their hearts breaking, they demand that the unity of the church be broken into segments that insure that they will not have to participate in any kind of Christian activity that is not exactly what they like.

And what is the difference between two cultures worshiping at different services because of preference and fear, and two cultures having lunch at different tables for the same reasons? Are we, as Christians, really trying to unite believers together, or are we just trying to tolerate one another in Jesus's name?

The sad truth of this is that, not only is this true of many Christians, but it is also true of too many leaders in the church today. God throughout scripture provides example after example of the truth that there is no unity apart from in Him, and that all those who attempt to find or construct a counterfeit man-centered unity will only cause undue and unnecessary separation of believers, not to mention a further alienation from the very world that they (the church) were established on earth by God to intentionally reach in His Name. Theologian J. M. Boice writes,

> It is not enough to merely understand and accept the gospel, as Peter did, nor even to defend it, as he did at Jerusalem. A Christian must also practice the gospel consistently, allowing it to regulate all areas of ... conduct.[46]

Throughout the gospels, there are numerous recordings of Jesus eating at the homes of sinners and fellowshipping (i.e., spending time) with people the religious scholars of the day found unacceptable. Jesus modeled the importance of breaking bread with those who are in need of the love of Christ. And as far as those who need Christ's love are concerned, there are no acceptable boundaries behind which the church may hide, as to do so is to preach a false gospel.

What if your church discerned the part of your city that God wants you to reach, and what if you started sharing meals and fellowship with the people there? If they speak Spanish, will you learn Spanish to reach them? If they are homeless, will you bring a card table and eat with them on the street? If they follow a different religion, will you lovingly extend patience and grace as they learn who Christ truly is through you? If they prefer a different musical style to yours, will you sing some of their songs with them? If they read a different Bible translation than you do, will you still investigate the scriptures with them?

The pursuit of unity in the church does not mean that we endeavor to have everyone conform to our own personal cultures, or to a culture that we may prefer but do not fully live out ourselves. The pursuit of unity in the church means that we are willing to sit at the lunch table with whomever God wants us to sit and eat with, no matter what anyone else may say or think. After all, we are talking about Christ culture.

---

[46] Boice, J. M. (1976). Galatians. In F. E. Gaebelein (Ed.), *The Expositor's Bible Commentary: Romans through Galatians* (Vol. 10). Grand Rapids, MI: Zondervan Publishing House.

CHAPTER 10

CHRIST CULTURE IS RESCUED FAMILIES TOGETHER IN A LARGER EMBRACE

It's important to realize that we adopt not because we are rescuers … We adopt because we are rescued.

—David Platt

Families don't have to match. You don't have to look like someone else to love them.

—Leigh Anne Tuohy

Adoption is not the call to have a perfect, rosy family. It is the call to give love, mercy, and patience.

—Hope For Orphans

Adoption carries the added dimension of connection not only to your own tribe but beyond, widening the scope of what constitutes love, ties, and family. It is the larger embrace.

—Isabella Rossellini

One of the most popular and enduring television shows of all time is the classic *The Brady Bunch*. While *The Brady Bunch* would air for just five seasons in the early 1970s, since the show went into syndication in September 1975, it has been broadcast on television somewhere in the world every single day.[47] At its core, the Brady Bunch was about a mixed family learning to live together, and perhaps that is what makes the show so relatable to people all around the world and across generations. Many people can relate to having a step-sibling or to being raised in a home without a mother or father for a period of time, if not for their entire childhood. An astounding 40 percent of children today are born to single mothers, and of that group, the vast majority of those children are born into Hispanic or African American households.[48] All told, the heritage of broken and/or "fragile families"[49] is one that is far too common in our culture today, and one that can be addressed, at least in part, through the church in Christ culture.

Christ culture, perhaps somewhat like the Brady Bunch, is life in a community that is made of people who have come together who were not part of one direct, singular family of origin. Again, Christ culture is many cultures brought together and living in one comprehensive culture (i.e., Christ culture). Taking the idea even further, Christ culture is very much a ministry of adoption.

It is quite possible that some of you who may be reading this book have had some kind of experience with adoption. Maybe you were adopted as a child, or maybe you have adopted a child, or you have tried to adopt a child at some point in your family life. If you have had any of those experiences, you will certainly appreciate the immense difficulty that adopting a child places on a family. If you have not had any experience with adoption, hopefully this chapter can give you a glimpse into the work of adoption, why it is so difficult, and why the church needs to intentionally take on the difficult work of adopting the lost and broken in their communities. To be sure, we are speaking of adoption in two different ways in this chapter:

1. For the purposes of the overall topical illustration, we will examine the process of adopting a child in a parental capacity,

---

[47] Rubin, Lawrence C., ed. *(2008). Popular Culture in Counseling, Psychotherapy, and Play-based Interventions.* Springer Publishing Company. p. 248.

[48] https://www.huffingtonpost.com/lavar-young/children-out-of-wedlock_b_868193.html. Accessed on 4-18-2018.

[49] Ibid.

particularly to highlight how difficult it is to adopt a child in the first place.

2. We will speak of spiritual adoption, which happens on two levels. The first level is through Christ's salvation and regeneration, and the second is when the local church adopts the believer as a part of their church family and cares for them accordingly.

It is essential to fully understand the gravity of what God is asking us to do as a church in America (and around the world). God is asking us not just to welcome visitors on Sunday, but to help them become adopted into God's family with the expectation that we will also adopt them into our local church family. The challenge for the church in this respect is that we have to overcome the negative inertia that has set in from decades and decades of relying on donuts, coffee, and an "engaging" and "relevant" Sunday experience to do that work for us. Make no mistake about this: welcoming a visitor for a Sunday is much different than adopting a spiritual orphan for a lifetime, but nonetheless, the latter is a part of our mission as the church.

With that said, it is certainly more comfortable and convenient to focus on making Sunday a great time because it does not require any kind of change from us for the rest of the week. Why would the church be so hesitant to truly adopt God's lost children if the church loves Him as much as they say they do? Well, the simple answer is that adoption is hard, and often frustrating and disappointing, and for many people, frustration and disappointment early on in any process are enough to tempt them to quit. But of course, when the church sticks with Jesus and is faithful to adopt His lost children, it presents a beautiful picture of our purpose in Him, both for now, and for eternity.

Why Is Adoption So Hard?

Speaking about a legal adoption of a child in America, there are a few reasons that make adoption one of the most difficult processes in which to endeavor. First, the question must be answered as to whether your home is fit to adopt a child.[50] In terms of legality, personal/criminal/financial background checks must be completed, the home must be inspected and deemed secure, social workers will make several home visits and conduct many interviews with the prospective parents, and many times there are things that the family learns they must do and/or change to be approved to be put on a waiting list to possibly adopt a child. To be sure, it is a good thing that such detailed verification and vetting occurs when considering the proper home for a child. A person's life is being directly affected by the choices of others, and that person (the child) is often unable to make any decision for his/herself, so the process, while incredibly detailed, thorough, and time consuming, is necessary. With that said, such knowledge does not make the process easier on the hopeful parents. Many parents wishing to adopt desperately want to do so to help a child in need of a home, but nonetheless, going through an adoption process is terribly stressful and both emotionally and physically demanding for the potential parents.

At the same time that hopeful parents work hard to make sure that their home is ready, the parents are also preparing for quite a considerable financial expense.[51] Depending on the type of adoption (i.e., adoption from an agency, adoption from foster care, etc.), the financial cost alone can threaten to break the spirits of the potential parents. And this is not to mention any legal fees, lawyers, agency fees, and should the parents be adopting a yet-to-be-born child, costs associated with the care of the biological mother as well.

Last, adoption is exceedingly difficult because it comes totally without guarantee.[52] A potential family could spend thousands upon thousands of dollars, while at the same time completely turning their lives and home upside down, be approved to adopt a child, and still not ever actually adopt a child. In some cases, adoptive parents have welcomed a new child into their home, only to have to give the child back when a biological parents reasserted their parental rights. And sometimes, whether the child is adopted or biological, the love offered

---

[50] Judith Wellen, *Why is it Hard to Adopt a Child?* Found on https://www.quora.com/Why-is-it-hard-to-adopt-a-child. Accessed on 4/18/2018
[51] Ibid.
[52] Ibid.

by the parents can ultimately be rejected by the child causing tremendous strain, hurt, and brokenness.

Certainly, adoption is not a work for those just "testing the waters" of parenthood. Adoption is a serious commitment to care for a child who would otherwise not have a home, let alone the love and guidance of parents who are able and willing to care for them. The adoption part of community is one aspect that does not get taught or demonstrated very often in the life of the American Christian church. We as the church simply do not connect the idea of making disciples with that of adoption. Yet again, throughout the scriptures, those who trust in the God of the universe inherit (or are adopted into) a life in God's family, which is the church. But too often, that process is broken because, while God is always faithful to adopt those who trust in Him into His eternal family, the church is not as faithful in adopting those same children into their local church family.

Adoption as Presented in the Bible

In the New Testament, such spiritual adoption is likened to a farming process called "ingrafting" (Romans 11:11–24). In Romans 11, the apostle Paul describes how Christ's salvation has come to the Gentiles and contrasts that with Israel's current state of unbelief in Jesus Christ as Savior. Furthermore, Paul points to a time when Israel will no longer continue in their unbelief and will at that time be grafted into Christ once again.

The physical farming process of ingrafting is actually quite fascinating. Essentially, ingrafting is where a stem/infant branch with a few buds on it is connected to the vine, root, or stalk of a pre-existing tree.[53] Both the branch and the stalk are cut in such a way that the vascular cambium tissue (the "veins") of each can line up and connect, thereby giving the branch access to the rich nutrients supplied by the

---

[53] Sherri Seligson, *A Scientific Look at the Branches, Vine, and Grafting in the Bible.* Found on http://sherriseligson.com/a-scientific-look-at-the-branches-vine-and-grafting-in-the-bible/. Accessed on 4/18/2018.

stalk. In fact, one stalk can support various kinds of fruit, provided that the fruits in question are related.

For example, an orange tree can support lemons, limes, and grapefruit, among its own native oranges, since all such fruits are citrus and are thereby closely related. Moreover, a farmer can take a healthy stem (branch) from an unhealthy tree and ingraft it into a healthy tree to save its life. Talk about the definition of evangelism, right? Just think of that concept for one second. One tree, supporting multiple fruits, some that came from healthy tress, some that came from unhealthy trees, all living together and sharing the same nutrients, and producing *all the ingredients* for a citrus salad at the same time. Would not that be a worthy goal of the church today? Such a picture is probably the single best visual example of what Christ culture is, and how, in Christ culture, the many cultures of the world can come together as one. Let's illustrate how this can apply to the church in America today.

For the purposes of this example, we will say that the American church is primarily oranges. We have oranges growing on the branches that are connected to the vine that is Jesus Christ. The oranges get their nutrients from Christ, who again, is the Vine (not our words, but His, in John 15:5). Now, let's say that God has impressed upon a church of oranges to reach out to a community of limes in their city. At this point, the church has three options.

Option 1, the church can obey their calling in their city, reach out to the lime community, and ingraft the limes into the Vine, which is Christ, and at the same time welcome the limes into their own "orange" church family.

Option 2, the church can reach out to the lime community, but instead of ingrafting them into the Vine, they can try to make the limes become oranges *before* they become a part of God's eternal family. This kind of outreach effectively says, "Yes, God loves you the way you are, but He won't accept you until you are like us."

Option 3, the church can come up with a litany of excuses as to why it is just not "the right season" to be reaching out to the lime community.

It would be an interestingly curious adventure to discover which of the above three statements/scenarios best describes the American Christian church today. What do you think? Of course, in faithfully obeying God's command to make disciples of all nations, the church faces two significant challenges when it comes to the adoption part of the work.

The first challenge the church faces is to resist the temptation to try to ingraft people into themselves as opposed to allowing the Holy Spirit to ingraft them into Christ. In our experience, many churches would line up well with option 2, in our impromptu survey. The reason is not that they do not want to reach their cities, but instead of the branches (i.e., people) being ingrafted into the Vine, they often try to ingraft the branches into other branches, usually themselves. While this does not lead to healthy fruit, it is understandable as to why such a temptation exists:

Simply put, we tend to think that we are the person God wants everyone to be.

Sure, we are not perfect; we recognize that. And we know that God has made each person uniquely and wonderfully, but at the same time, we gravitate toward those who *already* reflect our existing cultural rhythms, values, interests, and lifestyle. And should we encounter someone who does not reflect ourselves, it is difficult to resist the temptation not to try to shape them into another version of ourselves. But Christ wants us to be like Him, not like each other (that is evidenced in the fact that He created more than one person), and wherever we are like each other, it is because we are like Christ first in those areas of life.

The second challenge hearkens back to the challenges of adoption, whereas many people will flat out resist the word of God at every turn. And even if some people spend time in our churches, and with a healthy church family, they may still end up resistant and ultimately not be a part of the family of Christ. The work of adoption, whether in the practical or the spiritual sense, is a risk, no matter what, because while we as the church are responsible to sow the seeds of the gospel and to water and till the soils, we are not in charge of the harvest. In other words, we do not get to decide whether our extended love will be received. Just like parents who have children, there is no guarantee that the love of a parent will be received and/or returned by the child. The work of being God's ambassadors on earth is emotionally taxing, physically draining, and spiritually exhausting, but when God does bring a harvest, when lives are transformed by their connection and ingrafting into the Vine that is Jesus Christ, the work is so much more than worth it.

How Do We Know If We Are Ready to Adopt the Lost in Our Communities?

As we mentioned earlier, one of the reasons why state adoption agencies and social workers do such extensive research into potential adoptive family and their home is because they do not want to send a child into an unhealthy or otherwise unstable environment. It stands to reason that the same is true when it comes to ingrafting people into our church families, as they are ingrafted into the Body of Christ through His salvation. If our government, state, and social agencies care about the homes into which orphaned children are adopted, how much more so does Christ care about the condition of the churches into which His lost children are adopted?

To know if your church is ready to adopt the lost in your city, you need not look to anything more than what is motivating your mission among your church body. In Mark 12:29–32, Jesus says that the most important commandment is to "Love the Lord with all your heart, soul, mind, and strength … (and) to love your neighbor as yourself" (paraphrased). In recent decades, the American church has attempted to major on the latter, while assuming the former.

The "love your neighbor" command, while of significant importance, is not the correct motivation for our mission of reconciliation as the church. The first and most important command is to love the Lord Jesus Christ, and that first and most important command is also our motivation. Only an enthusiastic love for Christ can effectively inspire a lasting love for others, especially since there is no guarantee that the "others" will love you back. Furthermore, we are commanded to love the Lord in four specific ways: heart, soul, mind, and strength.

Our hearts, souls, minds, and strength as people are the things that mature as we grow. Therefore, our love for God in our hearts, souls, minds, and strength are expected and commanded to mature as we journey on the path of faith in Christ. Now, as you look to your church, or your own family, is there a maturity among you in those areas that inspires you, a group of oranges, to reach out to a group of limes and allow them to continue being limes while at the same time being ingrafted into Christ, and adopted into your orange church family? Your answer to this question will tell you whether your church family is mature enough to be a safe family for the lost in your city.

To be sure, allowing the limes to continue to be limes does not mean that their sin is tolerated, because all sin is not tolerated. What it means is that they continue to be who God intended them to be and that the harmony you have with one another is rooted in your unity in Christ as opposed to a unity of earthly culture. This is what Christ culture is.

Are you starting to see it now? Can you see your church living in Christ culture in your community? Are you beginning to think of the limes in your city that Christ may want you to reach in His name?

One Last Farming Thought before We Move On

The process of earthly ingrafting is limited to grafting fruits/plants together that are already of the same kind. In other words, ingrafting is limited to fruits/plants that are already related somehow. For instance, citrus fruits can be ingrafted with other citrus fruits, apples (which are a part of the rose family) can be grafted with other apples, and so on. This scientific limitation is consistent with the order of creation that God established, that being that one created thing cannot turn into another totally different created thing (i.e. primates did not turn into human beings). As a result, it would take being of one's own kind for life to be sustained (i.e., a deer cannot raise a human being from infancy; the human being would die).

The beauty of Christ culture flips that order on its head. Somehow, and in some way, God in His amazingness is able to work within the laws of creation that He established and transcend them at the same time. Let's imagine our churches as orange branches again. In the created world, you could not take the budding stem of an apple tree and ingraft it into an orange tree. But with and in Christ, we orange branches can be ingrafted into the same tree with apples, bananas, corn on the cob, sugar snap peas, and so much more. Why? Because the Vine we are ingrafted into as people is the Vine that sustains all life. We are quite right in our immediate thinking that we, as oranges, cannot sustain the lives of apples. But it is not us who sustains life. Rather, it is Christ and Christ alone who does so.

Perhaps when we, as the church, will fully recognize that we are just as rescued by Jesus as we hope the lost around us will be, maybe then we will be more consistent in making disciples of Christ, instead of trying to make copies of ourselves. And as such, when God asks us to go into our communities and reach these people or those people, they do not have to look like or act like us to fit in with us because it is not our job to make them fit in with us, nor is that God's goal. Our job is to bring them the love of Christ, and then hopefully they, just like us, will be in grafted into Jesus Himself, just as we are, and in that way, we can worship together, serve together, love each other, and truly live in Christ culture.

CHAPTER II

CHRIST CULTURE IS HUMAN CULTURES TOGETHER BECAUSE OF GOD'S TRUTH

To a true child of god, the invisible bond that unites all believers to Christ is far more tender, and lasting, and precious; and, as we come to recognize and realize that we are all dwelling in one sphere of life in Him, we learn to look on every believer as our brother, in a sense that is infinitely higher than all human relationships. This is the one and only way to bring disciples permanently together. All other plans for promoting the unity of the Church have failed.

—A. T. Pierson

One of the most important characteristics of any organization is the culture in which said organization operates. Of course, to this point, we have discussed the importance of the different cultures of our cities coming together in Christ, and now we will look at what kind of culture our different cultures will produce if we are faithful to God's revealed word as the body of Christ. It is essential that any culture found within a church body be expressly and exclusively rooted in God's word if the people who make up the congregation are to have unity and love among each other.

A vital question that is asked of any leader or leadership team has to do with the kind of culture they want to establish in their organization.

An organization can have any kind of culture its leadership desires to establish, but without question, an organizational culture will emerge, whether intentionally or not. For every organizational culture in society, that culture is established by the company leadership. For example, some organizations have a team-style culture that puts the needs of the team, both practically and philosophically, at the top of the decision-making chain. For example, Netflix has implemented a very team friendly unlimited family leave policy, giving its employees more flexibility and peace of mind in terms of caring for their own families.[54] In theory, this showing of support for the team member inspires the team member's care for potential customers since the team member knows that he or she is cared for and valued by their leadership. Other organizations take on a more horizontal, or "flat," kind of culture wherein every team member is an equal, though their responsibilities and roles within the organization differ.[55] Certainly, there is also a traditional, hierarchy-style culture that is perhaps the kind of culture most often characterized in American business and corporate society today.

The American church is also an organization (albeit, much different than a business corporation), and as such, the church will adopt the culture set forth by its leadership. However, unlike corporations and businesses, the church's leader was, is, and will always be God. And what's more, since God is the leader of the church, God has also already established the kind of culture He wants for His people. The challenge for the American church is to obediently engage in the culture God has previously established, as opposed to trying to establish a "new" culture with each and every new local church.

To be sure, this does not mean that individual churches are not shaped by the people God places in leadership and/or the total congregation itself. Rather, it means that the culture God initially established for His church needs to be the filter through which the human elements of culture, which may or may not become a part of the local church, are measured. In other words, Christ culture should dictate how human cultures interact, relate, and worship in the local church. Assuming

---

[54] Cassie Paton, *5 Types of Corporate Culture: Which One is Your Company?* Found on https://blog.enplug.com/corporate-culture. Accessed on 4/23/2018.
[55] Ibid.

that Christ culture is in the driver's seat in that regard, there is plenty of liberty and freedom in Christ for the individual local church to have its own specific traits and characteristics thereof. And we know that prejudice and discrimination will not be a part of this culture because they are already not a part of Christ culture.

Granted, engaging in Christ culture can be easier said than done. After all, one of the reasons prejudice is so difficult to overcome is because oftentimes that prejudice has been wrongly justified (i.e., people finding excuses to discriminate by misinterpreting dcripture) and thereby embedded in the normal practices and routines of any particular person or group. Nonetheless, God, through the Bible, has given us a series of commands and prescriptives to help us be able to live in Christ culture, in spite of our natural pride, prejudices, and sin. To illustrate this, we are going to do a kind of fill-in-the-blank exercise that will prayerfully help us to better recognize the important distinctives of Christ culture that Jesus has already established, and with which we need to engage if Christ culture is going to become a reality in the American church.

Christ Culture Is a Culture Devoted to Worshiping God Together (Acts 2:42)

There have been countless books, blogs, sermons, and songs about the early church as described in Acts 2, and the plethora of information is much needed. There is exponential value in going back to the roots of things and examining what the first intentions were, and how said intentions were carried out. What we see in the first descriptions of the church is how devoted they were to worshiping God together. Through hearing the teaching of the Bible, spending time with one another, and being known in their communities as a people who follow Jesus, celebrational/ceremonial meals, and prayer the early church gathered together to worship Jesus in these corporate expressions.

A devotion is something that requires an outpouring of affection of energy from one person in another person or thing, depending, of course, upon the receiver of said devotion. So for a person to be devoted to something, it would mean that person puts his or her energies, affections, and emotions into partaking with and pleasing whatever or whomever it is to which they are devoted. The challenge that has always faced Christians in being able to live out this basic principle and intention of Christ culture is that instead of the believers being devoted to worshiping God together, today, many Christians have fallen into a spiritually anemic pattern of wanting their church to be devoted to themselves. As a result of this, we as the church, as opposed to gathering together as the church to read God's word and praise Him and His truth, go to church to hear a sermon that we hope is entertaining (but not too entertaining), theologically deep (but not too lengthy), personally inspiring (but not too convicting), and specifically personally relevant to whatever our immediate felt need might be at the time. And of course, when our church does not live up to this standard, we write a note on a comment card, and we find an online article about how our church is "doing it wrong" so we can post it on our social media pages and have all of our friends "like" our current mini-crusade.

And when we demand that our church be devoted to us, it means that instead of being a part of a church body that is known for the bold obedience of the Christians there, we look for a church that is known for catering to the opinions and preferences of its own membership. The celebrational meals should be fitted to our own specific desires as well. And instead of praying with the believers for the needs of each other and their city, we look for a church that will pray for us first. In a previous chapter, we talked about how our love for God is our first motivation for obeying Him and accomplishing His purposes for our lives, and in the same way, it is our devotion to God that needs to be our first motivation as a community of believers. If we hold ourselves at ransom, wanting the church to be devoted to us individually, we will never experience Christ culture as God has intended it. Instead, we will experience a counterfeit culture as humans have repurposed it.

Inasmuch as Christians can mistakenly put the emphasis of devotion on themselves, we can also be devoted to the wrong things and/or people as well when it comes to the church. Consider the experience of Paul and Barnabas in Lystra, found in Acts 14. The two missionaries taught and healed people, at which the crowds began to worship Paul and Barnabas as gods (Zeus and Hermes, respectively—Acts 14:12). As soon and Paul and Barnabas realized what was going on, they mourned intensely, tearing off their own clothes, and tried to teach the people that there is only one God and that they (Paul and Barnabas) were humans, just like everyone else. Unfortunately, the words of Paul would fall on deaf ears, and the people, having been cheered on by a group of Jews who had recently joined them, stoned Paul and left him for dead outside the city.[56]

While the crowds at Lystra came from a pagan background, their response to their new-found idols' (Paul and Barnabas) refusal to accept their worship is not wholly unlike the response of some Christians today who, whether purposefully or not, make idols of their favorite pastors and/or church leaders and respond viciously when those leaders disappoint them, or are eventually replaced. Devotion, then, is a powerful emotional and spiritual focus that truly cannot be set upon the wrong recipient without inevitable letdown and discouragement. We must continually be reminded of the fact that there was, and is, only one perfect leader who is worthy of that kind of worship and devotion, and that leader is Jesus Christ. This is also why it is so critical that Christ culture dictate our local church cultures. When the order is reversed, and we give our devotions to a wrong vessel (whether a person, a music style, etc.), we end up more like Christ's crusaders than Christ's disciples, and the last time we checked, Jesus wanted believers to be His disciples.

How Do We Know If We Are Devoted to Worshiping God and God Alone?

In keeping stock of where are devotions lie, we can examine the kinds of things that offend us most deeply. While such a suggestion may sound somewhat counterintuitive—that is, looking to a negative to discern a positive—it is reasonable to submit that the things that offend us the most will reveal those things/people to which/whom we are the

---

[56] Of course, Paul would be restored to health, and he would later write about this experience in his second letter to the Corinthians.

most devoted. For example, think of the kinds of things that might encourage you to join, or leave, a particular church. What things come to your mind? Do you think of things like the music? The preaching? What about their children's ministry? Having served in local church ministry for a combined thirty-five years, we have heard just about every reason there is for joining and/or leaving a church. Granted, some of the reasons are unavoidable, such as when a family moves away. Very few of the reasons had to do with the devotion of the believers to God, and/or their obedience to God's mission for the church. What kind of a difference do you think churches would make if the believers who attend chose their churches based on a fidelity to God, and a faithfulness to God's mission for the church, as opposed to the subjective quality and frequency of the programming and conveniences that may be offered by any given church?

Christians choose to join churches for all kinds of reasons: theological stances, preaching style, denominational affiliation(s) (or lack thereof), kids' programs, music style, Bible translations, type of facility, and so much more. At the same time, within our church bodies, we are often greatly offended over the very same things, exposing how devoted we are at that time to that person or thing. When it all comes out in the wash, the bottom line is this: you will know if you are devoted to worshiping and knowing God together with His people if Christ alone is enough for you. In other words, if your church could not promise you your style of music, preaching you liked, children's programs, comfy chairs, indoor plumbing, coffee and donuts, time to shake the pastor's hand, a comment card for your spiritual gift of critique, and whatever else you may desire—if all your church could offer you was Christ and Him crucified—would that be enough? Could you endure singing songs that you do not like, knowing that what your church is doing is true, accurate, and faithful to God's truth and mission for the church?

Being devoted to God first, as the early church in Acts was, means that we measure the quality and effectiveness of ministry and our church through the lens of Christ, and Christ culture, not our preferences. Being devoted to God first means that when we come to worship God, we are coming to give Him praise for how wonderful He is, and for who He is, instead of coming to church for what we get out of it.

Being devoted to God means knowing that God has *already* given to us abundantly through the death and resurrection of Jesus Christ, and that alone, with no other blessing or security, is enough, and worthy of my sacrifice of praise to Him. We mentioned earlier that to be devoted to something means that we pour out of ourselves into whatever it is that might be the object of our devotion. When it comes to our devotion to Christ, how often do we consider what we are willing to give to/for Him, as opposed to how much we want Him to give to us?

Many Americans know how devoted they are to their spouses and families because of how much they are willing to give up for their benefit, and how much we are willing to sacrifice to show them how much we love and value them. Do we, as Christians, show even a fraction of that kind of devotion to God? Many Christians take time away from church to be with their families, but how many Christians take a life pause with their families to be with God? How will you know what kind of devotion you have to God? You'll know by whether Christ alone is enough for you, and by whether Christ alone is worth it to you.

As we continue this journey of Christ culture distinctives, we will see that even the order of the distinctives in their presentation in scripture was not an accident. Clearly, if we are going to be effective on our God-given mission, we must first be wholly devoted to the mission-giver, who is God Himself. A community of Christians that is devoted to worshiping God together is the first essential element of Christ culture.

Christ Culture Is a Mutually Sacrificial Culture (Acts 2:44–45)

Because the early church was first devoted to God and the worship of Him together, they were able to enjoy unity of purpose and love through Christ as well. This unity and love in Christ would compel the Christians at this time to richly sacrifice so other believers in their church family could have their needs met. Moreover, the early church was mutually sacrificial in that they did not sacrifice for each other expecting a return (that would be a loan). Rather, they were "all in" together.

It is an often-tendered objection to God-centered Christianity that, if a church does not exist first to meet people's needs, then the church will not be effective at meeting any needs period. However, what Acts 2 shows us is that a prior, uncompromised devotion to Christ is what inspires the following sacrifices. It was precisely because the early church did not attend church for selfish, momentarily emotionally needy reasons that the church was able to meet each other's needs so comprehensively. In fact, the account in the book of Acts literally says that no one among the early church had needs for very long because the Christians there were so eager and willing to sacrifice however necessary to supply for everyone's needs at the time (Acts 4:34).

Is it not significant that a me-first approach to being a part of the church will result in stingy hands and closed fists, yet a God-first motivation will result in generosity beyond anyone's furthest expectations? Here again, these are not aspects of culture that people established on their own. These are the culture aspects established by God and carried out accordingly and sensitively by His people. Thus, the practice of generous sacrifice is a curious thing. For those who do not have a vibrant relationship with God, the tendency is to see sacrifice itself as the best way to please God, and so it happens that many Christians will sacrifice for God to win His favor and blessing (which is not for sale, by the way). But when we love God first and foremost, and when we apply the truth that God said in 1 Samuel 15:22–24, that obedience is better than sacrifice, we find that God uses our sacrifices for the benefit of others, as His favor is given to us in response to our faith in Him and obedience of Him. Furthermore, God established that our sacrifice was not how we "get to God," but how God got to us, and that was done in the life, death, and resurrection of Christ. In Christ culture, our sacrifices do not necessarily change God's mind about anything, but God uses them to help change the hearts of those we minister to in our cities.

Christ Culture Is an Actively Personal Culture (Acts 2:46)

In Christian methodology circles, a popular buzzword (as of the time of this writing) is "community." The word and method of "community" has grown out of the idea that the church has become stale and academic (i.e., impersonal) and that society as a whole has become increasingly fragmented and isolated, leading to a critical need for human-to-human interaction and connection. Such a spiritual and cultural diagnosis is arguably accurate, and it is good for the church to recognize the growing chasm between people that is created by such a hyper-individualistic culture as is currently found in America.

And so it is that this aspect of Christ culture—that is, being actively personal—is one that is readily embraced as necessary by many American Christians. However, if we are looking at the early church as an initial example of what such a community of believers looks like, we will see that the relational and community aspects of Christ culture flowed out of the early believers' sole devotion to God and their mutually sacrificial obedience to Him. Perhaps the greatest hurdle facing the church today in effectively implementing this distinctive is that we often put the proverbial cart before the horse, so to speak.

It is common for churches today to focus so steadfastly on inspiring a church community environment that is conducive to real relational connection that they lose sight of the Greatest Commandment ("love God first with all that you are, and love others as yourself")[57] and the Great Commission ("make disciples of all nations").[58] The problem here is that when, as a church, our greatest love is each other, we tend to run out of momentum at some point because we are missing our primary motivation, which comes from loving God first. Just like how our greatest motivation for our mission as the church is our love for the Messiah, our greatest motivation to love each other is the love we have for Christ Himself.

As the early church in Acts demonstrated, their primary devotion to and love for God compelled them to sacrifice for one another out of obedience to Him, and this mutual sacrifice led to meaningful and

---

[57] Matthew 22:36–40
[58] Matthew 28:19

lasting daily relationships. If we desire authentic community as a church in our cities, the only way such a thing can be sustained is if our devotion to God and resulting sacrifices further compel us into relationship with each other. Why is this? Simple. People let us down; God doesn't.

About two years ago (at the time of this writing), America's favorite television dad, Bill Cosby, was outed as a serial rapist and sexual predator. Virtually all of America had, for more than four decades, celebrated Bill Cosby as a beacon of wholesome, family entertainment, and as an inspiration to millions of Americans. If you were a Cosby fan like us, you remember how much of a disappointment it was to hear of his transgressions, and it became more difficult to go on appreciating his work in the same way because the enormity of his deceit overshadowed his brilliant body of work. In fact, the only way a person could go on to have any compassion for Bill Cosby at all was if they could see him in the way that Christ sees him.

People constantly let us down because no one is the person we make them out to be in our minds. And without a prior love of Christ that breaks our heart over sin, when a person lets us down (which they inevitably will), it will be exceedingly hard to love them and/or respect them again. Because of sin we all have hurt the ones we love, and we all have sinned against one another and against God. In that light, apart from a preexisting devotion to Christ, people are virtually unlovable. But because God first loved us, we can first love Him, and as a result we can then extend His love to those around us, even when we do not have any love within ourselves to give.

The early church in Acts is recorded as a people who got together in each other's homes every day. *Every day.* What kind of love do you think you need to have for people if you are to see them and spend time with them *every* day? And when we spend that kind of time, and share that much life with other people, we are bound to not only come upon their faults and sins, but we will likely have conflict and hurt with them as well. Without the love and forgiveness found and offered only in and through Christ, there is no way that a true, authentic community can last. But if we follow the example of the early church, seeing that our engagement with God and His mission will lead to engagement with each other, we can experience this aspect of Christ culture in a real and sustaining way.

The Authenticity of Christ Culture Is Recognizable to Outsiders (Acts 2:47)

As the description of the early church comes to a close in Acts 2, the author (Luke) notes that the early believers enjoyed the favor of the people in their city. The early church was so devoted God and faithful to His mission for them that the people could see that these "followers of the Way" were the real deal. Later in the book of Acts, the people begin to turn on the church and become hostile toward the new church, but nonetheless, the people of the city could not deny that this new church lived out the truths they preached. In other words, the early church walked the walk and were not shy about it.

One of the things that challenges the credibility of the church in cities across our nation is the idea that Christians do not really practice what they preach, if they even understand it to begin with. The Bible demonstrates a people who love God, love each other, and show that love through obedience and sacrifice, and yet when many churches are visited each week, what people read in the Bible and see in real life today are two different things. What is seen in many American churches today is either a rigid fundamentalism that opposes any and all outside influence/experience or programs that rely on gimmicks instead of grace to get the message of gospel across. Granted, there are churches that fall in the middle of the spectrum, but with the ever-increasing swing of the cultural pendulum, fewer and fewer are found in that area of ground.

More and more we find church conferences promising new and innovative ways of reaching our communities, and we see books upon books and articles upon articles about the latest method of communicating the gospel and why that way is the "best" way, etc. It would appear that to the lost and dying world, the church looks schizophrenic when it seems that the church would rather pursue temporary cultural trends that present the gospel of the living Christ. If Christ is indeed enough, why do churches feel the need to make Him somehow culturally exciting and relevant? If Christ is enough, should not Christ *already* be exciting and relevant? Do our new and improved empirically studied ministry methods really enhance our ability to obey our mission, or do they distract us from it? In our celebrity-fixated culture, do we obey because our favorite online pastor just told us to or because Jesus *already* to us to?

As the church, we have to remember what the lost in our country have seen from us over the past 120 years. Our country saw the rise of fundamentalism in the 1930s. They witnessed the church fight *with herself* (let alone the national civil rights movement) about the basic rights of people with different skin tones. They witnessed the church wage a multi-decade battle against gay marriage, citing the sanctity of marriage, yet at the same time remain virtually silent as the overall divorce rate climbed to 50 percent (granted, both divorce and homosexuality are sins, but hopefully you can see why this might look like a confusing position to the lost in our country). They see politically conservative Christians donating millions of dollars to pro-life political candidates, yet two-thirds of women who have had an abortion say that they experienced exclusionary and/or dismissive treatment from the church *while they were still pregnant.*[59]

The truth is that the church has plenty of opportunities to demonstrate to their cities that we are who the Bible says we are. But the lost in our communities need to see *us* carrying out God's mission firsthand, not our politicians or our programs. Even outspoken atheists like magician Penn Jillette will admit that they respect Christians who are serious about living out their faith, even though they do not agree with Christians at all.[60] It is not too late for the church to return to Christ culture, and for the ripple effects of Christ culture to be seen positively in our cities and neighborhoods.

---

[59] Lisa Cannon Green, *New Survey: Women Go Silently from Church to Abortion Clinic.* Found on https://www.care-net.org/churches-blog/new-survey-women-go-silently-from-church-to-abortion-clinic. Accessed on 4/24/2018.
[60] https://churchpop.com/2016/01/16/atheist-penn-jillette-christians-evangelize/. Accessed on 4/24/2018.

Christ Culture Is the Only Lasting Force for Good the World Has Ever Seen

If we look through the prism of history, we will see nations rise and fall. World organizations and institutions have been birthed only to eventually and inevitably fall away. We have seen a variety of economic systems be tried to varying degrees of success or failure. And we have seen world leader after world leader promise a better world, only to leave office or die before their personal utopias can be fully legislated. Yes, we have seen all these things come and go in the name of the betterment of humanity, yet none ever achieve such a goal, and none last forever— none, that is, except for the Christian church.

It is almost absurd to think that the church is such an effective force in the world, but it is, and we would do well as believers to remember that. The church has no official earthly nation to call home. Rather, the church is made up of people from every nation. The church does not sell a product for profit, yet it has survived because of the obedient generosity of those who comprise its population. No matter how illegal Christianity has ever been, the Christian church grows in spite of worldly hostility and hatred. No matter how much society tries to erase God from the public square, the church still persists, carrying the gospel of life in Christ to the lost wherever they are.

For the American church specifically, we need to recognize that the culture barriers that have kept us apart for so long are robbing us of the good we could do in our country in obedience to God, for the good of the people of our communities. Many cities in America have several churches in their midst, yet few of those churches actually serve and minister together, and what's worse, sometimes they are competing against each other. The fact that in the face of entire civilizations emerging and disappearing, the church has remained is staggering, humbling, and hopefully compelling.

It is staggering because the church has no physical armed forces to defend herself, yet all attempts to eliminate the church by force have failed the world over. And just that fact alone is humbling to think about because it shows just how God is protecting His children as they journey through a world that hates them, which begs the question, why do we persist in journey through this hostile world as divided as we are as a church? And hopefully it is a truth that will compel us Christians to get back to our first love and back to our mission of reconciliation.

The book of Titus is pastoral letter written by the apostle Paul to a new pastor, Titus, who is going to Crete to minister to the believers there. Paul spends the first two chapters of the letter giving Titus instructions on how to appoint elders in different parts of the city, and how the church members are to treat each other. In chapter 3, Paul highlights some traits that the church should avoid as it endeavors to be faithful to God. Notably, the things Paul highlights in this section are all things that tend to divide the church, and seeing as Christ culture is human cultures worshiping God together, it would do us some good to briefly look at these divisive patterns to avoid as we return to our journey following Christ in Christ culture.

CHAPTER 12

CHRIST CULTURE IS NECESSARILY UNITED, NOT UNNECESSARILY DIVIDED (TITUS 3:1-11)

> Satan greatly approves of our railing at each other, but God does not.
>
> —C. H. Spurgeon

The apostle Paul begins chapter 3 encouraging Titus to remind the believers in Crete that they need to be respectful of their governmental authorities, and that they should "be ready" (v. 1) to help in the efforts of their city leaders when those efforts are for the good of the community.[61] This was to help demonstrate the fact that the Christian church is the force for good in the world that it was designed to be. Being "ready" for the good works in the community, in part, meant that, instead of a community of people who constantly grumble about their city leaders and are, as a result, unenthusiastic about their community, they were to be actively looking for any and every opportunity to benefit the people of their city.

In verse 2, Paul turns the instructions to a focus on the pagan neighbors of the community. The Christian church is not to have a

---

[61] Hiebert, D. E. (1981). Titus. In F. E. Gaebelein (Ed.), *The Expositor's Bible Commentary: Ephesians through Philemon* (Vol. 11). Grand Rapids, MI: Zondervan Publishing House.

habit of slandering, (i.e., cursing, talking negatively about), the lost in their city. From firsthand experience, this is a battle that the church is fighting to this day, that is, resisting the temptation to speak poorly of the lost in their communities. In our time in ministry, we have heard Christians take the condition of the lost so lightly that it is clear that the peril of their (the lost's) souls are of little concern. Furthermore, a constant drumbeat of negative criticism of the lost in our communities will result in us, as church bodies, isolating ourselves away from them, which is the opposite of our mission to reach them.

As Paul continues in verse 2, he calls on believers to be a peaceful people, considerate and gentle toward others. It is a revealing exercise to hear what people complain about. Certainly, as a group, a given church can be generally considerate and peaceable, but what about individually? When we consider others in our communities, do we consider them as more important than ourselves and serve them accordingly? Or are they in our way as we go about our very important business? To consider others, we must take the time to know where they are coming from, or at least give them the benefit of the doubt that they are not out to ruin our day specifically. Do we, as Christians, regularly take enough time to know enough about the people of our neighborhoods to be able to consider them at all?

I heard a story once of an elderly man who was out for a Sunday drive with his wife of many, many years. The old couple were driving on a two-lane road, very slowly, and another car pulled onto the road behind the couple. The car behind the couple was late to work, and in a hurry, and not surprisingly became irritated at the elderly driver.

As the two cars drove on, the driver in the rear car continued to mumble obscenities and curses at the elderly couple in front him, as it seemed that no matter where he wanted to go, the slow old couple were always in front of him. As the driver of the rear car approached his place of work, he noticed that the elderly couple were headed to the same place.

As it turned out, the impatient driver was an orderly at an assisted living home for elderly people, and the elderly man was taking one more Sunday drive with his wife who was to be admitted to the assisted living center that day. But because of impatience, and being inconsiderate, the orderly who was late to work (which, by the way, was not the elderly couple's fault) missed an opportunity to rejoice and mourn for a couple who had spent their whole lives together and who were now being forced apart due to the strains and pains of just getting older, and all they wanted was one more Sunday drive together. Isn't it interesting how being inconsiderate will inspire in us a lack of gentle treatment of others, which will in turn prevent a peaceable attitude and atmosphere of life for all involved?

While the above story is an anecdote about people you do not know, what about the people you do know? Whether they are lost or saved, how considerate are you with them? Do you see the connection between being considerate and being gentle and peaceable? The apostle Paul calls us to be peaceable, considerate, and gentle toward each other. And isn't that kind of culture a culture you would want to be a part of? That's Christ culture.

As Paul continues in chapter 3, he spends several verses on the motivation for this kind of culture, which is, as we have stated, love for Christ and gratitude for His mercy that was given to us, even when and even though we did/do not deserve such grace, love, and life. Since we have discussed this point in some detail, we will journey forward to Paul's final word of caution to Titus in chapter 3, which is to avoid foolish disputes over past traditions and/or scripturally baseless opinions. Paul literally calls such things useless and notes that the fruit of these kinds of arguments is a divided people, which is a tragedy, because that means that the church has become divided over a useless matter.

Here again it is worth asking, "How many churches in America are divided because of useless matters?" And what does that look like to a watching world when we, who are supposed to be united in Christ, split over the stubbornly held opinions of a few people? The apostle Paul says that this kind of division is so toxic that those who are stirring said division should be removed from the church.

As if we needed another example, here in Titus 3 we have a demonstration of the truth that unity cannot be found in the agreement of people. Rather, unity is only found in the truth of Christ. If we are more concerned about affirming our opinions than we are about submitting to Christ's lordship in our lives and in our churches, then our barriers of division and cultural wars will only continue, and we will lose the valuable time that we have in the freest nation on earth to spread the good news of the gospel that brings all nations together and overcomes the bitterness and malice that can develop between us. Author Jay Adams writes,

> Few things are sapping the strength of the church of Jesus Christ more than the unreconciled state of so many believers. So many have matters deeply imbedded in their craws ... between themselves and other Christians. They can't walk together because they do not agree. When they should be marching side by side through this world... they are acting instead like an army that has been...fighting among themselves. Nothing is sapping the church of Christ of her strength so much as these unresolved problems... There is no excuse for this sad condition, for the Bible does not allow for loose ends. God wants no loose ends.[62]

Paul, in the middle section of Titus 3, talks about how we all were separated at one time, and how we all hated each other. And yet, Paul writes, when Christ came in kindness and love, He saved us from that life, so why would we want to continue in a life of division and hatred? Why would we look to find new ways to separate what Christ died and rose again to bring together? As Americans, we live in a country that is the envy of the rest of the world. People from all nations come here for a better life, and we believe that the best earthly life possible is found here in America. Now, with the nations of the world descending upon our great land, will we see this as a mere political immigration problem, or as an opportunity to win the nations to Christ, and to adopt them into Christ culture? God is bringing the nations to our neighborhoods and doorsteps. We can answer the door and invite them in. We can welcome them to our neighborhoods and adopt them into our spiritual families just as they are adopted into Christ if/when they are saved. The opportunities are upon us, the time is now, and the choice to obey is yours.

---

[62] Jay Adams, *Christian Living in the Home*, P&R Publishing, 1972, p. 35–36. Found on https://gracequotes.org/topic/conflict-church/. Accessed on 4/24/2018.

CHAPTER 13
BRINGING IT ALL TOGETHER

Has it ever occurred to you that one hundred pianos all tuned to the same fork are automatically tuned to each other? They are of one accord by being tuned, not to each other, but to another standard to which each one must individually bow. So one hundred worshipers meeting together, each one looking away to Christ, are in heart nearer to each other than they could possibly be were they to become unity conscious and turn their eyes away from God to strive for closer fellowship. Social religion is perfected when private religion is purified.

—AW Tozer

As we mentioned at the beginning of this book, this is not a how-to book on the church and race relations, or a new methodology for reaching cultures that are different from your own. This book is written with the hope that it will renew the minds of Christians across this country who have been fighting the culture wars on the world's terms instead of from God's truth. This work is not "how to" in its initial design because, quite simply, we do not know the cultures that surround you and your church family specifically. It will take your prayer and strategic effort to engage with the cultures in your city to determine what the best course of action may be for your particular church body. Having said that, we want to bring all of this information together and provide you with a jumping-off point, so to speak, so that you can begin the all-important, God-given work of reaching the nations, starting with the ones represented in your community.

The entire first half of this book was dedicated to showing you, however briefly, where much of our modern-day thinking concerning race/cultural relations finds its roots, so we can adequately address these mischaracterizations of and about humanity with the unchanging truth of God. The second half of this book was dedicated to outlining some of the foundational and initial characteristics and distinctives of Christ culture, which is the human culture that, through our faith in Jesus, we are adopted into in this life as we grow in Christ with His body the church, and that we look forward to in eternity to come. Our mission of reconciliation is a difficult one primarily because it is not a person's default instinct to want to identify with Christ in the first place. Furthermore, once a person receives salvation through Jesus, he or she is then to die to him or herself—that is, die to the things of this earth and live unto God, which again runs antithetical to that natural inclinations of humankind. Yet this is the work in which we, the church, have been assigned the role of Christ's ambassadors before a lost and dying world.

It is our sincere prayer that you will take time to examine how you have been approaching the different cultures God has brought into your world to discern whether you have been seeing different people as the world presents them, or as God sees them. We pray also that you will grow in your desire to see all people become who God wants them to be, and that a person's cultural differences can be understood as one part (personally significant, but not personally definitive) of God's grand design. Christ culture is not many cultures merely coming together in one common space, all the while remaining separated by their respective cultures. Christ culture is many cultures coming together, worshiping God, and loving each other as one totally new culture: Christ culture.

APPENDIX

Getting Started

As we have examined the myths surrounding our modern perceptions of cultures, race, ethnicity, etc., and as we have taken stock of the core tenants of Christ culture, it is important to put the wheels of God's truth and justice in motion in our lives. Again, while we cannot offer to you specific steps that are guaranteed to work in your unique community, we can suggest some starting points upon which you can begin to effectively bridge the culture chasm in your city through your local church. The following tips are compiled from the Christ culture companion small group/individual study guide.

1. **Be confident in God's intention for created humanity and know how to back it up from the Bible.**

   The book of Genesis provides a storehouse of information regarding God's intentions for humanity, how we are to live with one another, and how we are to relate to one another. With a virtual never-ending tidal wave of cultural information supplied by modern historians, media, and so on, it is critically important for the Christian to carefully consider scripture's account and demonstration of God's intent for humankind to best understand the truth about your own creation, and the creation of those who are different than you.

2. **Know the difference between culture, nationality, ethnicity, and race.**

We cannot treat people equally if we do not understand why all people are equal in the first place. Moreover, we will not treat people equally if we continue to see each other in different classes of humanity, be those classes racial, economic, or otherwise preferential.

A culture is the traditions, values, and customs found among any particular group of peoples. Cultures are usually separated by geographic region, whether within a larger continent and/or country, or within a given individual city.

Nationality has to do with the earthly location in which a person is originally from, or has earned/obtained/received citizenship. Ethnicity is the micro-culture that exists in the various cultures around the world. For example, what most Americans would understand as Indian-style cuisine is one aspect of a broader culture within a nation.

A race is what has been commonly used as a catch-all word that means all of the above. However, biologically and biblically speaking, there is only one race of people and that is, all people. It is a sad truth, however, that while race is not in fact a biological reality, racism is certainly real and has been at the core of many a human atrocity over the course of world history. Racism is hatred built on nothing more than biological fiction.

3. **Find ways to learn about different cultures in your community so you can reach them intentionally.**

One of the best ways to learn about the values of a culture is to invest in the children of that culture. Many churches have youth ministries in their buildings, but few churches have ministries to youth in their communities. Engaging with the youth in your city is a great way to understand the different cultures in your community.

Joining local civic organizations can connect you with many of the local leaders in your community, and that will bring an enriched understanding of your city to your church. For years, it seems like the church has wanted only their pastor to do this work, but it is high time for the whole church to get involved in these ways.

4. **Challenge yourself not to make preconceived assumptions about people who are different than you.**

    Take the time to hear their stories, and to learn what experiences they've had that lead them to the worldview that they may have. Just because someone has brown skin does not necessarily mean that he or she is ethnically African or Hispanic, etc., and just because someone has lighter skin does not necessarily mean that he or she is ethnically European Caucasian.
    Make it a point to learn who people truly are before you assume to know what's best for them in their current situation.

5. **Try taking a break from striving for political solutions in Washington, DC, and start sacrificing for personal solutions right where you live.**

    People are more than a political demographic and can be spoken to without the slogans of our favorite politicians getting in the way.

6. **Ask God to show you if there are any people you directly or indirectly discriminate against, and repent at the Holy Spirit's prompting.**

    The only way discrimination and prejudice can truly be wiped out is if it is overwhelmed in the hearts of those who harbor such hostilities.

7. **Find one thing you enjoy doing that can serve people in your city directly, and figure out how to do it.** You can even invite some friends to serve with you, and it does not have to be your pastor's idea. You can do it!

8. **Pray for the good of people you dislike.**

    Christians are very good at pointing out what's wrong with people, but we rarely pray for those people. Do not fall into that trap. Consider people you don't like as God's way of asking you to pray for them—even if you don't know them. Pray for the good of those you dislike, or even hate. God will honor your prayers in His way and time.

9. **Strive to follow the example of the early church in Acts and the instructions of the apostle Paul in how you treat your fellow church family members.**

10. **Pray for the American church as we go forward into a new era of culture as a nation.**

    As we mentioned in the introduction to this book, if our nation sees us treating people in the ways that God wants us to, and seeing them in the way that He does, we will likely be ridiculed even more. All of us, together, need to pray for one another, that God will give us all the strength, courage, endurance, and boldness we will need if we are going to faithfully live in Christ culture as a people of God.

THANK YOU

Pastor Jay and I would like to thank you for taking the time to read this book. We pray that these words will be used by God to help you and believers across our country approach the culture divides in a way that is consistent with what God has revealed in the Bible. And it is our sincerest prayer that you were encouraged and inspired to at least take one step individually, and with your church family, in bridging the cultural divides that exist in your community. As a church, we are strongest when we are united, and the only unity we have is in Christ.

Let's make that a reality together.

Join us at ChristCultureOnline.com and continue the conversation and the journey toward unity in Christ.

In Christ Alone,

Pastor Jay Scutt and Pastor Andrew Southwick

BIBLIOGRAPHY

Bergman, Jerry. *Birth Control Leader Margaret Sanger: Darwinist, Racist, Eugenist* found on https://creation.com/margaret-sanger-darwinian-eugenicist. Accessed on January 22, 2018.

Boice, J. M. Galatians. In F. E. Gaebelein (Ed.), *The Expositor's Bible Commentary: Romans through Galatians* (Vol. 10). Grand Rapids, MI: Zondervan Publishing House. 1976.

https://www.brainyquote.com/topics/racism_3. Accessed on November 24, 2017 at 9:43pm PST.

https://www.britannica.com/topic/multiculturalism. Accessed on 4/25/2018.

Cannon Green, Lisa. *New Survey: Women Go Silently from Church to Abortion Clinic.* Found on https://www.care-net.org/churches-blog/new-survey-women-go-silently-from-church-to-abortion-clinic. Accessed on 4/24/2018.

Carson, D. A. Matthew. In F. E. Gaebelein (Ed.), *The Expositor's Bible Commentary: Matthew, Mark, Luke* (Vol. 8, p. 227). Grand Rapids, MI: Zondervan Publishing House. 1984.

Cerullo, Megan. *California Woman Refuses to Sell Home to a Trump Supporter,* found on http://www.nydailynews.com/news/national/california-woman-refuses-sell-home-trump-supporter-article-1.3907232. Accessed on 4/12/2018.

https://churchpop.com/2016/01/16/atheist-penn-jillette-christians-evangelize/. Accessed on 4/24/2018.

Cole, Nicki Lisa. The Sociological Definition of Race. Found on

https://www.thoughtco.com/race-definition-3026508. Accessed on January 8, 2018.

Davis, John J. *Paradise to Prison: Studies in Genesis*, Sheffield Publishing; Salem, WI, 1998. Pp. 88-89.

https://ferris.edu/HTMLS/news/jimcrow/what/. Accessed on January 24, 2018.

Gaebelein., F. E. Sailhamer, J. H. Kaiser, Jr., W. C. Harris, R. L. & Allen, R. B. *The Expositor's Bible Commentary: Genesis, Exodus, Leviticus, Numbers* (Vol. 2). Grand Rapids, MI: Zondervan Publishing House. 1990.

Ham, Ken and Ware, A. Charles. *One Race One Blood*, (Green Forest, AR; Masterbooks), 2013. pp. 22-23.

https://www.huffingtonpost.com/lavar-young/children-out-of-wedlock_b_868193.html. Accessed on 4-18-2018.

Johnson, A. F. Revelation. In F. E. Gaebelein (Ed.), *The Expositor's Bible Commentary: Hebrews through Revelation* (Vol. 12). Grand Rapids, MI: Zondervan Publishing House. 1984.

Lauderbach, Preston. *Memphis Burning* found on

https://placesjournal.org/article/memphis-burning/?gclid=EAIaIQobChMIwfiqxdDx2AIVTG5-Ch1L3AnUEAAYASAAEgJSO_D_BwE. Accessed on January 25, 2018.

Moral Majority, found on Britannica.com/topic/Moral-Majority, accessed on April 5, 2018.

Paton, Cassie. *5 Types of Corporate Culture: Which One is Your Company?* Found on https://blog.enplug.com/corporate-culture. Accessed on 4/23/2018.

Rubin, Lawrence C. ed. *Popular Culture in Counseling, Psychotherapy, and Play-based Interventions.* Springer Publishing Company. p. 248. 2008.

Rupprecht, A. A. Philemon. In F. E. Gaebelein (Ed.), *The Expositor's Bible Commentary: Ephesians through Philemon* (Vol. 11). Grand Rapids, MI: Zondervan Publishing House. 1981.

Seligson, Sherri. *A Scientific Look at the Branches, Vine, and Grafting in the Bible.* Found on http://sherriseligson.com/a-scientific-look-at-the-branches-vine-and-grafting-in-the-bible/. Accessed on 4/18/2018.

Smietana, Bob. *Sunday Morning in America Still Segregated – and That's Ok With Worshipers* found on http://lifewayresearch.com/2015/01/15/sunday-morning-in-america-still-segregated-and-that's-ok-with-worshipers/. Accessed on 11/9/17.

Wellen, Judith. *Why is it Hard to Adopt a Child?* Found on

https://www.quora.com/Why-is-it-hard-to-adopt-a-child. Accessed on 4/18/2018.

Wong, Alia and Fattal, Isabel. *The Complicated History of Affirmative Action: A Primer* found on https://www.theatlantic.com/education/archive/2017/08/the-complicated-history-of-affirmative-action-a-primer/535707/. Accessed on January 25, 2018.

SCRIPTURES (ALL SCRIPTURES NIV 2011, UNLESS OTHERWISE NOTED)

Referenced but not directly quoted:

Genesis 1:27
Genesis 2:23–25
1 Samuel 15:22–24
Matthew 9:14–17
Matthew 14
Matthew 16:13–20
Matthew 22:36–40
Matthew 25:40
Matthew 28:19
Mark 2:21–22
Mark 6
Mark 12:29–32
Luke 5:33–39
Luke 9
John 6
John 14
John 15:5
Acts 2:42
Acts 2:44–45

Acts 2:46
Acts 4:34
Acts 10
Acts 11
Acts 14:12
Acts 15
Romans 11:11–24
Romans 12:1–2
1 Corinthians 3:16
2 Corinthians 5:11–21
2 Corinthians 6:16
Galatians 2
Galatians 3:28
Ephesians 4:14
Titus 3:1–11
Philemon
1 Peter 2:9
Revelation 21:1–6

Directly Quoted

Matthew 8:14–16
Matthew 22:13–22
Acts 17:26
Romans 10:12
Romans 12:2
Galatians 3:28

Ephesians 4:24
James 1:13–15
Revelation 21:3
Revelation 21:4–5
Revelation 21:6

Printed and bound by PG in the USA

USA2018PGIL